GRIZZLIES AND GRIZZLED OLD MEN

GRIZZLIES AND GRIZZLED OLD MEN

A Tribute to Those Who Fought
to Save the Great Bear

Mike Lapinski

FALCON®

GUILFORD, CONNECTICUT
HELENA, MONTANA

AN IMPRINT OF THE GLOBE PEQUOT PRESS

A FALCON GUIDE ®

Copyright © 2006 by Mike Lapinski

Text design: Lisa Reneson

Library of Congress Cataloging-in-Publication Data
Lapinski, Michael.
  Grizzlies and grizzled old men : a tribute to those who fought to save the great bear / Mike Lapinski.—1st ed.
    p. cm.
  Includes bibliographical references.
  ISBN-13: 978-0-7627-3653-9
  ISBN-10: 0-7627-3653-4
  1. Grizzly bear—Conservation—United States—History. 2. Wildlife conservationists—United States. I. Title.
  QL737.C27L3395 2006
  333.95'9784—dc22
                              2006004810

Manufactured in the United States of America
First Edition/First Printing

THIS BOOK IS DEDICATED TO THE MEMORY OF
HOWARD COPENHAVER, MY FRIEND AND MENTOR
AND A GREAT ADMIRER OF THE GRIZZLY.

CONTENTS

The author and The Globe Pequot Press assume no liability for accidents happening to, or injuries sustained by, readers who engage in the activities described in this book.

PREFACE

I seen me a big grizzly back in the 1950s. Ol' Jack Horning and me were elk hunting up in the North Fork of the Coeur d'Alene River. We come around a corner on an old logging road and there the ol' boy stood, not more than 30 yards away. Oh, he was a big brute! He was a perfect silver-tip. He huffed and bounced stiff-legged at us and popped his teeth. Jack was gonna shoot him, but I told him not to. We just backed off and let that ol' bear wander into the brush. It's nice to know there's a few animals out there that ain't afraid of man.

—Lester Smith
Red Ives Ranger Station, North Idaho

Unfortunately, not all men, before or after Lester Smith, have shared his opinion. The first recorded meeting between a white man and a grizzly bear ended typically—with a dead bear, as noted in *The Journals of the Lewis & Clark Expedition*. The following decades didn't get any better for the great bear. Settlers and ranchers moved into grizzly country and depleted bears' natural food sources, forcing them to take an occasional cow. As a result stockmen and state governments, along with the federal government, embarked on a century of sustained eradication—using guns, traps, poison, and fear—to push the grizzly to the verge of extinction in the West.

PREFACE

Once totaling somewhere between 50,000 and 100,000, only a few hundred bears survived in the most remote, rugged mountainous areas. And still the killing continued. Whenever a grizzly bear was spotted, hunters, hounds men, and trappers descended upon the area in a macabre show of bravado to lay claim to killing the last grizzly. With bear numbers so low and public sentiment so overwhelmingly against the grizzly, some naturalists went so far as to declare the bear virtually extinct in the lower forty-eight states. Only a miracle would save the great bear.

Yet in the midst of this unprecedented carnage, winds of change began to blow. Daring men stepped forward and questioned the accepted public opinion that the only good bear was a dead bear. Through the printed word and through their actions and deeds, these men spread a new gospel—that the universally vilified, feared, and loathed grizzly bear was instead a noble beast worthier of our admiration than a bullet through its heart.

This change in men's hearts took root in a most unexpected source. Grizzly Adams, a brutal bear trapper and sideshow exhibitor of California's giant grizzlies in the mid-nineteenth century, came to love the great beasts he once tortured. He took to sleeping with them and voiced regret for his misdeeds before he died. Then the great bear hunter, William Wright, who authored a book about his sordid exploits, wrote of his grudging admiration, and regret, for all the grizzlies he'd killed. Our great sportsman/conservationist president Theodore Roosevelt not only wrote about the lordly presence of the grizzly, but he also staved off its extermination by creating and enforcing laws to protect the last few great bears in our national parks.

Long before professional biologists developed a strategy for proper human coexistence with the grizzly, French Canadian Bud Cheff learned from his Salish Indian friends while roaming Montana's wild Mission Mountains in the 1920s, "You no bother'um Sumka (Salish for "grizzly"), Sumka no bother'um you." Bud's life among the last free-roaming Indians and his acceptance of the grizzly as a treasured animal, became a gospel that he preached—not only about the majesty of the bear but also the nobleness of Indians.

PREFACE

No one brought the plight of the grizzly bear to the public eye more vividly than Frank and John Craighead, whose pioneering bear studies in Yellowstone were broadcast into our living rooms via black-and-white television in the 1950s. We watched with bated breath as these irrepressible brothers scrambled back to their pickup mere seconds ahead of an angry grizzly that had abruptly recovered from sedation. But the Craighead brothers weren't in it merely for entertainment. Their pioneering use of radio collars to study and track grizzly bears ushered in today's scientific era of bear management.

These men, plus a number of others—some famous, some not—stood in the gap and courageously halted the fusillade of bullets, traps, poison, and poor policy in their circles of influence to staunch the flow of innocent blood and bring the grizzly back from the brink of extinction.

They're old now, these men who once were young and virile, strident of step, and keen of wit. Their eyes have grown dim, their shoulders stooped, their gait slowed. And some—Adams, Wright, Roosevelt, Frank Craighead, and Howard Copenhaver—have passed from among us. But for a season their hearts and spirits burned with an unquenchable fire to preserve this great lumbering beast. Thanks to them the flame of conservation and preservation of the grizzly glows brightly today.

Consequently, *Grizzlies and Grizzled Old Men* is much more than an epitaph for old men's deeds in days gone by. A new breed of honorable men and women have stepped forward to stand in the gap for the great bear. Leaders like Chuck Bartlebaugh, whose Center for Wildlife Information is resolutely determined to educate the public about proper behavior in bear country, or Carrie Hunt, who helped develop bear pepper spray and who now saves numerous grizzlies each year by administering aversive conditioning to problem bears with her Karelian bear dogs. And then there is the irrepressible Doug Peacock, whose impassioned writing prompted a generation of nature lovers to look upon the great bear with affection and respect—even if those emotions are not reciprocated by the bear.

PREFACE

Thanks to a generation of grizzled old men and to those men and women who courageously follow in their footsteps, this book serves as a reminder to all of us that we can make a difference.

CHAPTER 1

✦━❉✦❉✦━✦✦━❉✦❉✦━✦✦━❉✦❉✦━✦

THE GREAT BEAR ERADICATION

The big sow grizzly hurried down the forested trail but paused long enough to throw her snout skyward, sniffing loudly. The sweet odor of decaying flesh once again reached her nostrils and set her belly to grumbling. Since emerging from hibernation two weeks ago, she had eaten only some dry grass and bark from a few saplings.

The tantalizing odor made her want to gallop forward, but her three cubs were hanging back, play-fighting and snooping under rocks and logs. At any other time, she would have encouraged their play and foraging. Now, she uttered a deep grunt of impatience. The startled cubs scrambled close to her.

At a bend in the trail beside a creek, the odor became over-powering, and the sow loped ahead to a pile of fresh-cut logs. At the base of the log pile she found the hide and guts of a deer. The sow stepped forward, mouth agape to devour the food. Suddenly she felt a sharp pain in her right leg. For a moment, she stared down, confused by the strange thing fastened to her paw. Then she smelled the steel.

A furious bellow ripped through air, knocking the frightened cubs backward. The sow lunged to escape the massive no. 5 Newhouse bear trap, but the heavy device stayed securely fastened to her paw, even though she dragged two eight-foot logs attached to the trap with heavy chains some 50 feet down the trail. Soon the logs became entangled in a thicket of small trees.

The sow turned her fury on the trap and bit it so hard that her upper canine teeth broke. The pain, at first bothersome, became maddening as the trap bit deeper into her flesh with every frantic lunge.

For three hours the sow was a whirling dervish of bellowing, fighting, roaring, tearing fury until at last she lay back, exhausted. The cubs timidly approached her to nurse, but the sow pushed them away and returned to biting at the trap. By sundown, her lower canines and all of her molars were cracked or broken.

The next day was a torturous blur for the sow, by now almost mad with pain and thirst, and the pitiful wailing of her hungry, frightened cubs. Then came night, then day; and night and day. The pain eventually was replaced by a numbness in the paw, which had swelled to twice its normal size as a mixture of blood and lymph oozed from deep cuts made by the steel jaws.

On the morning of the fourth day, the sow was startled awake. She heard and smelled something. She reared up to her full height of seven feet, the big bear trap dangling from her right paw, and spotted the man cautiously approaching. The sow laid back her ears and lunged, but the trap held her fast.

In his book *The Lochsa Story* Bud Moore reported:

> Trapper Wes Fales laid the sights of his rifle between the sow's eyes. The rifle's blast echoed through the narrow canyon, and the sow collapsed. As Wes cautiously approached the inert bear, three small cubs hopped onto a large spruce log and hesitantly approached their mother. They sniffed the sow and began to wail, looking first at the man, then at their dead mother.
>
> Fales's first thought was that this was his lucky day. Besides the bounty and the price of the sow's hide, he'd make good money if he could capture one of the cubs. He tore off his wool jacket and dove at a cub, managing to

latch onto a tiny rear leg, then rolled the crying, biting animal in his shirt and stuffed it into his backpack. He hurriedly *peeled* the hide off the sow and left the oozing carcass and two other cubs behind as he trudged down the trail. All in all, it had been a good day, with more bear traps yet to check. But the cub wailed pitifully throughout the journey, and Wes Fales felt a pang of remorse—a dangerous emotion for a man determined to do his part to rid that corner of Eastern Idaho and Western Montana of every grizzly bear.

THE INVASION OF GRIZZLY COUNTRY

Historians estimate that as many as 100,000 grizzlies roamed the western landscape during the Lewis and Clark Expedition, ranging as far south as the Mexican Rockies, up through the Southwest and California, across the Great Plains of Texas, Kansas, and Nebraska, and spreading north through the upper plains and Rocky Mountains and west into Washington and Oregon.

Though Lewis and Clark's exploration of these lands west of the Mississippi made the nation aware of its potential, serious settlement did not begin for several decades. We need only skim their journals to understand why. Even the Corps of Discovery, which was actually a highly disciplined military detachment, armed to the teeth and always on the move, barely escaped the frontier with their lives. The journey was filled with the dangers of the wild country, whether rattlesnake bite, or disease, or hunger. Or a grizzly bear.

The Journals of Lewis & Clark, while read with interest by the people on the east side of the Mississippi, were also an intimidating set of documents that discouraged all but the most adventuresome folks with a yen for a new life in a brave new world. Those few who ventured west in the next three decades often disappeared, leaving relatives to wonder whether the missing brother or father had grown weary of writing, or was reduced to bleached, gnawed bones on the sun-baked prairie.

It wasn't until the 1870s that the trickle of western expansion became a flood. Massive movement of restless, land-hungry settlers in wagon trains poured into lands in the Southwest, where grassy prairies spread untouched as far as the eye could see. Settlers moved up through Utah, Colorado, and the Dakotas and into Montana. Others continued over the Rockies to the fertile agricultural lands of California, Oregon, Washington, and southern Idaho. Occasional Indian uprisings flared but were quickly extinguished.

These westward traveling people were predominantly farmers and ranchers. They brought horses and cows and pigs and sheep along with them to provide food and extra income. By the tens of thousands, settlers spread out and claimed isolated plots of land. Most of these early homesteads were within a few days' travel of population centers, enabling settlers to bring their crops and livestock to market.

It was still a wild land, relatively untouched by civilization, with its predator population intact. As soon as the chickens spread out to peck at grasshoppers in the scrub beyond the barnyard, coyotes and bobcats snatched them up. Wolves found cattle and horses to be easy prey, and even an occasional hungry grizzly came visiting.

Much has been written about the cruelness of the early settlers, but it should be remembered that these were a frightened people whose lives and whose children's lives depended upon milk from the cow, eggs from the chickens, and meat and money from the sheep or cattle. To lose even one cow might prove disastrous economically; to lose the entire herd put a family's existence in peril. As a result they did whatever was necessary to ensure the welfare of their loved ones. At the time there really was no other way to deal with the predator problem than to eliminate it.

Killing is not easy for most human beings unless certain criteria are met. Self-defense is one. Instinct takes over when a person's life, or the life of a loved one, is threatened. But self-defense killing is a short-term reaction to an immediate problem. To eliminate the source of the problem takes a mind-set that produces a sustained effort. The

Hides of a female grizzly and two cubs in Arizona, 1907

ROSCOE WILLSON COLLECTION, COURTESY OF THE ARIZONA HISTORICAL FOUNDATION

single-minded effort of the United States government to subdue the Native American was to dehumanize the Indian to the point where society as a whole felt the world would be a better place without them. Thus the sentiment: "The only good Indian is a dead Indian." It worked very well. Grown men who cuddled their babies and attended church felt not one pang of guilt shooting an Indian man on sight or thundering into a sleeping Indian village at dawn for a massacre of women and children.

The predator problem was approached with the same zeal. The grizzly bear, because it was big and ferocious when provoked, was considered a threat to the livelihood and personal safety of every man, woman, and child, and consequently deemed evil. The grizzly bear had to go. Infrequent bear attacks on humans were headlined in newspapers, along with atrocious stories of bears killing scores of cattle and sheep. With the taming of the Indian, it didn't take much prodding for the predominantly farming and ranching populace to adopt a policy of eradication toward the grizzly.

The near-extermination of an estimated 100 million buffalo in the West in little more than two decades by market hunters is well documented. Actually, it was relatively simple, due mostly to the herding nature of these dim-witted beasts the habitat of which was restricted to open grasslands. The big predators such as the mountain lion, gray wolf, and the grizzly were a different matter. The lion by nature is a secretive animal and seldom seen, even when plentiful. The wolf proved cunning and quickly learned to stay out of sight during daylight hours. And the great bear was difficult to find because it lived mostly in dense cover and rugged mountains, and it possessed none of the dim-wittedness of the buffalo.

However, there was a vast difference between the mountain lion and wolf, and the grizzly, in the mind of the average settler. The mountain lion seldom stood its ground when confronted by a human. The wolf garnered even less respect and came to be considered nothing more than vermin, a large version of the lowly coyote, which killed by night, then slunk back to its hole come daylight and cringed like a coward when cornered. The grizzly, on the other hand, proved its fearsomeness over and over again when cornered, often fighting ferociously to its last breath against hopeless odds. And not just fighting, but sometimes even winning, tearing the life from some brave or foolhardy human soul who had made the fatal mistake of pursuing a grizzly.

The demise of the grizzly would not be as easily accomplished as the wolf. To eradicate an animal as powerful, dangerous, and reclusive as the grizzly would take a determined effort by dedicated men who used American ingenuity, technology, and resourcefulness to reach their goal. One other thing was needed: to vilify the great bear to the point where the only good bear was a dead bear.

THE GREAT BEAR ERADICATION

THE SLAUGHTER BEGINS IN CALIFORNIA

Looking at the metropolis of Los Angeles today with its population of 50 million, it seems laughable to call this sprawling concrete jungle prime grizzly habitat. Yet, in its natural state it was a fertile land that produced a plethora of native fruits, nuts, and berries, and plenty of grass to feed thousands of elk, deer, and antelope, and a variety of lesser animals. It is estimated that upwards of 10,000 grizzlies roamed southern California alone when the first Spanish explorers appeared in the early 1800s. Not only was the California grizzly abundant, it also grew to massive proportions due to the abundance of food. Specimens topping 1,000 pounds were not unusual, and a few tipped the scales at 1,500 pounds.

Before the more sophisticated Spaniards arrived, Native Americans lived in fear of the grizzly because they had only primitive weapons to counter the sudden fury of a charging bear. With the Spaniards came the gun, and the grizzly bear finally found a human it would fear. Spaniards took large numbers of grizzlies, sometimes for sport, other times to keep their stock safe. However, historical accounts from the book *The California Grizzly* reveal that the Spanish approach was to leave the great bear alone if it wasn't bothersome.

Long before the Southwest became suitable for American settlers, California was well established, due to the abundance of valuable sea otters for the fur trade, whale oil, and the fertile valleys in the south. Thousands of immigrants from the eastern United States took the long six-month boat trip around the Cape of Good Hope to California. In May 1846 Spanish Governor Pio Pico wrote, "We find ourselves threatened by hordes of Yankee immigrants who have scaled the summits of Sierra Nevada with their wagons and penetrated the fruitful Sacramento Valley. Already they are spreading themselves far and wide, cultivating farms, vineyards and sawing up lumber."

As early as 1848 a census claimed there were 7,500 Spanish Californians, 6,500 "foreigners" (Americans), and 4,000 civilized former mission Indians. Of course, this was the calm before the storm.

THE GREAT BEAR ERADICATION

In 1848 gold was discovered at Sutter's Mill, and Americans poured into the state.

With the coming of the Americans, the Spanish live-and-let-live philosophy toward the grizzly evaporated. The American penchant for submission and domination of the land put the average American at odds with the grizzly. Ranchers and farmers almost immediately began ridding their valleys of the bear for crimes such as grazing on their grass or swiping honey or the occasional cow.

Much of the West was still uninhabited when professional California grizzly hunters were notching scores of kills. Jedediah Smith, famous scout and trapper, was the first American to note the presence of grizzly bears in California. While beaver trapping in the Sacramento Valley in 1828 he wrote, "I saw a Grizzly Bear and shot at him but did not kill him." John Work and a hunting party in the Sacramento Valley killed forty-five grizzlies between November 1832 and May 1833. George Nidever killed forty-five bears near San Louis Obispo in 1837, and Nidever claimed to have killed about 200 in previous years. William Gordon of Yolo County killed nearly fifty bears in one year in the 1840s. And three hunters in the Tejon Pass region in 1854 are said to have killed 150 bears in less than one year.

Farmers and ranchers paid these men to kill bears on their lands, and the bear meat was sold to hungry immigrants and later to gold miners. Then a curious demand sent these men to the hills to bring grizzly bears back, not dead, but alive.

The Spanish custom of bullfights created a brisk demand for large grizzly bears to fight the bulls, and a handsome sum, often $100 or more, was paid for a live grizzly ready to fight. But bringing a grizzly bear to market alive was no easy chore. Vaqueros occasionally succeeded in roping a bear, but this practice proved extremely hazardous to both man and horse. Eastern Americans who brought their woodworking crafts with them began building live bear traps made from stout logs, which resembled a small log cabin. The bear, lured by the smell of putrid cow guts, entered the trap, and when it pulled on the bait, a heavy door slammed shut. Sometimes the bear was able to dig under the walls and escape or was big enough to tear the trap apart. But if it was still there when the owner checked his trap, a team of horses dragged a heavy steel cage in front of the log cabin trap, and the enraged grizzly was transferred to it.

Spanish bulls were rangy, half-wild beasts weighing up to 2,000 pounds. Many who watched one of these hoofed demons trotting around the arena immediately put their money on the bull. The grizzly, when prodded into the ring, ignored the bull and sought a corner, or dug a hole to hide in, further heightening the hopes of the spectators who had bet on the bull. Before long, the bull lowered his head and hurtled his powerful bulk at the bear—whereupon all who bet on the bull lost their money.

The grizzly usually took the bull's initial charge full in the chest, which knocked the bear on its back, whereupon the grizzly clamped its jaws on the bull's head and wrapped its paws around its neck. While the bull was held in that position, the bear had its way with its powerful jaws wreaking havoc on the bull's head.

The bull, suffering intense pain and bellowing horribly, was unable to gore the bear and could only make a series of frantic efforts to free himself. Sometimes the bear suddenly wrenched the bull's neck to the side and broke it.

Jose Arnaz, a merchant in Southern California in 1840, told of a bear that "killed three bulls, one after another. When the bull approached, the bear thrust a paw in its face, or caught a leg in its jaws. In this way the bear forced the bull to lower its head, and when it bellowed, caught it by the tongue. It was then necessary to separate the contestants quickly to keep the bear from killing the bull immediately."

Another bear/bull fight occurred in Mexico with "Samson," a massive California grizzly captured by Grizzly Adams (see chapter 2). Albert Evans recorded the fight. "I saw the bear dig a hole big enough to hold an elephant. Samson then latched onto the bull with its paws as if it were an infant and carried it to the pit. It hurled it into the pit head first and slapped it with its wicked paws until half the life was knocked out of the bull. Then, holding the bull down with one paw, proceeded to bury it alive."

THE GREAT BEAR ERADICATION

As California evolved from a wild frontier society, public outcry against bear/bull fights forced authorities to ban them. The demand for live grizzly bears waned, but the demand for dead ones continued, oftentimes for sport and bragging rights to having killed the biggest known grizzly in those parts.

THE GRIZZLY IN THE SOUTHWEST

When the Civil War ended, the U.S. government sent an army of hardened war veterans to the West, and most Indian hostilities were extinguished with murderous efficiency. Settlers began to move into these territories, with Army troops leading the way to mop up the occasional pocket of hostile Indians. Troops often encountered grizzlies not accustomed to men, and these unlucky bears were often caught out in the open, offering great sport for men bored by the tedium of frontier life. With the grizzly, however, sport often turned into a fight for survival, as noted by Captain James C. Hunt, First Cavalry, who left Fort Apache, Arizona, with five men to check on Pueblo Indians:

> Early in the morning, just after the party had crossed the Rio Colorado Chiquito, on the bank of which they had passed over an open plain that rose in slight undulations covered with sage brush and scattered scrub oak, they spotted an immense bear about a mile ahead. The bear, upon seeing the men, turned and began running towards the mountains eight miles distant at the most ungainly gait imaginable, but when tested by the speed of the horses proved that at least for some distance a horse at full speed can hardly keep up.

By permission of Captain Hunt, the troopers Captain Fuller, Corporal Hyde, and Private Armstrong took off after the bear. With their horses in good condition and spurred on, it still took 4 or 5 miles to catch up with the galloping bear. The men were armed with Spencer rifles and revolvers, with the exception of Captain Fuller, who carried only a heavy revolver. At 30 yards, the men opened a lively fire, with little effect on the bruin. However, it is not so easy for men riding at full speed to hit such a crazily bounding animal.

Captain Fuller finally succeeded in sending a ball through the bruin's hind leg. The effect was to cause the bruin to run on three legs while holding his right hind leg off the ground, crimsoned with a free flow of blood, which amazingly did not slow it down that much. If anything, the bear increased its speed for a distance, but the wound soon began to tell, and after gaining some distance, the bear turned to bite at his wounded leg.

A shot from Corporal Hyde's carbine again cut him across the ham. The whole party, keeping up their fire, closed to about 20 yards of the bruin, when he whirled and bounded toward Corporal Hyde's horse. The corporal spurred the horse on, but the bear soon overtook the horse and caught it by its flanks. The poor horse gave one desperate kick, for an instant throwing the bear off, but in a second the bear pulled the horse down on his haunches and with one swipe of its paw, sent Hyde flying off the horse. The horse galloped off wildly, while the corporal, without any weapons, was rolling on the ground struggling for his life with the bear.

Captain Fuller and Armstrong reined in their horses, while within 3 yards of their horses' feet was this enormous bear ferociously biting and tearing the limbs of the unlucky corporal. The men's weapons were empty; and while they reloaded, Corporal Hyde struggled manfully, striking with his fists and legs and arms down the mouth and throat of the bear, while his own blood ran in streams from his wounds.

The bear rose twice on its hind legs, standing much above the corporal's head, and the two literally wrestled as two men would in a championship match. The wounded leg of the bear was Hyde's salvation, for the claws in the brute's hind feet would have torn out his entrails. In ferocity and wildness nothing could surpass the horrible appearance of this brute, with bloody foam dripping from its jaws, while the poor man called pitifully to the party to help him for God's sake or he would die.

Armstrong, believing there was still a load in his carbine, jumped off his horse and, placing the muzzle of his piece against the side of the bear, pulled the trigger, but it only snapped. The next instant the bear was tumbling Armstrong, biting and tearing him as it had done with Hyde, who was lying covered with blood a few feet away. It looked as if both men would receive mortal wounds before the others could assist them. Captain Haley finally rammed a load into his revolver and fired it at the bear. The ball must have cut him, for he bounded away with his leg held up and headed for the mountains. The two injured men were a dreadful sight, with pale faces, streams of blood running down them, and their clothes torn to shreds. Corporal Hyde, though suffering greatly, only said, "Here's my carbine, kill the d——d beast for me, Captain, for God's sake."

While another troop moved up, Captain Fuller and Haley reloaded their carbines and did their best to make Hyde and Armstrong as comfortable as circumstances would allow. They then remounted and took after the bear, which was making its way to the mountains, stopping occasionally to turn and lick at its hindquarters. The horses, pushed to the run, soon overtook the bruin. At a safe distance the men fired their carbines repeatedly. After a few attempts by the hobbled bruin to get at the horses, he turned at bay under a scrub oak, evidently unable to go further, but still ready to fight. The bear's vitality was so great that a dozen more deliberate shots were required, each passing through some part of his body, before his head dropped and he expired.

After such a hair-raising account in the newspaper, it's not difficult to imagine the reaction the average settler might have when he spotted a grizzly bear peacefully grazing on a distant ridge. With thoughts of the blood-thirsty demon descending upon his family, his first reaction was to empty his rifle at the beast.

Also penetrating the western mountains were miners seeking gold. When a strike was made, usually far beyond the trappings of civilization, men of every description flooded into those areas to seek their fortune. Most were ill-equipped, and there were scant rations available locally to keep them alive. Meat hunters, crusty old men roaming adrift since the glory days of the great buffalo slaughter, spread out from these mining camps to procure meat. And the menu often included grizzly bear.

A meat hunter wrote in his journal:

> Yesterday Mr. Fuller and myself went out with our guns for a short hunt near the mining camp at the south end of the Santa Rita Mountains. A mile from the camp, we saw a large cinnamon bear about 600 yards away leisurely walking, taking an occasional bite from a cactus. We crept softly forward until we were a hundred yards distant.
>
> The bear must have got wind of us because he began snuffing the air and tossing his head . . . it was a critical moment, and I felt we were standing on dangerous ground. Fuller, being the best shot, leveled his gun and fired. He struck the bear for it gave an awful grunt and reared on its hind legs and looked in every direction for its enemies. When he failed to see us, he became frightened and started to move off. I took courage at this and fired my sharp shooter at him, but this only made him run faster. We tracked him by his blood for about a mile and then gave up the chase. If we had come upon him suddenly it might have cost us our lives.

Areas of the West near forts and mining camps quickly lost their bear populations to meat and sport hunters, though the influx of men affected only a fraction of the bear population. It wouldn't be long, however, before the war against the grizzly expanded to a whole new level.

In the early 1870s large cattle ranches bankrolled by Eastern investors took over vast expanses of grasslands. Immediately there were depredation problems. Most of the predators doing the killing were mountain lions and wolves, though a few head of stock were also taken by grizzlies. However, the grizzly's penchant for putrid flesh made him only too happy to take over a week-old cow carcass baking in the hot sun, and that is what the ranch foreman often discovered when he went searching for the missing cow. Grizzlies were shot on sight, and large ranches employed a number of professional hunters.

Most of these hunters were old reprobates—decaying descendants of bygone days of the fur trade. They jumped at the chance to make good money on the lucrative bounties offered for mountain lions, wolves, and bobcats. Many of these men were eccentric, and some were simply deranged.

James "Bear" Moore fell into the latter group. An account submitted by government hunter J. E. Hawley related how two government trappers, while afield in the Black Range of west-central New Mexico, heard the horrible bawling of a bear in pain. The men crept forward and spied Moore taking a white-hot iron rod from a fire and sticking it into a hole in a cabin bear trap that held a grizzly. Moore gleefully rammed the heated rod into the bear's flesh, giggling and slobbering as the tormented bruin screamed in pain. Moore, having been mauled and his face horribly mutilated by a grizzly he'd wounded, wreaked his own horrible vengeance on any bear he trapped, torturing it for hours with hot metal rods before tiring of the excitement and shooting it.

Fraud was common among bounty hunters, with many wolfers (former mountain men and trappers who pursued wolves for profit) pen-raising wolf pups dug from dens, breeding them, then killing and turning in their scalps for bounty. Still, bounty hunting became so much a part of outdoor life in the Southwest that the Arizona Territorial Legislature passed a bounty act that authorized counties to appropriate monies for predators as small as the coyote. Of course, the grizzly unfairly took the brunt of the blame for depredations caused by wolves and fetched the highest bounty, sometimes reaching $300—more than a full year's salary for most men.

Overgrazing of grasslands and severe drought bankrupted most of the big ranches, and oftentimes cattle were left to starve to death or die of thirst. Grizzlies, having taken to the mountains to escape the market and bounty hunters, fell into the habit of slipping down from the high country to feast on the carrion that littered the landscape.

Upon these abandoned ranchlands arrived droves of settlers anxious to claim the up to 640 acres offered by the Homestead Act of 1848. The big ranches had expected some losses of stock to depredation, and the disappearance of up to a dozen cows during the course of the year was usually shrugged off as part of the price of open-range cattle ranching. But to the settlers and small ranchers who spread out over these defunct big ranches, the loss of even one cow was unacceptable. What ensued was a wildlife war stretching from Texas to Montana, during which no quarter was given to any predator.

Cattle associations sprang up in almost every county throughout the West, offering bounties and sometimes employing hired hunters to rid the land of vermin. By 1880 most counties in the West offered some sort of bounty on mountain lions, wolves, and bears. Hunters employed traps, both leghold and cabin, as well as hounds. Of course the wolf and mountain lion, being secretive animals, were usually long gone before these hunters showed up in response to a rancher's complaint. That left the grizzly, lying contentedly on the rotting cow carcass. But any hunter who thought the pudgy bear would be an easy kill learned quickly, sometimes at the cost of his life, that a riled grizzly was nothing to mess with. Hound hunters also discovered that, besides losing many dogs to the grizzly when it was brought to bay and turned on them, a chase was not always successful, with about one bear killed for every five chases, which might last two days or more.

Predator numbers dropped, but the problem never went away because of the vastness of the wilds beyond the ranchlands. Though millions of dollars were spent in more than a decade of bounty hunting, livestock depredation continued at an unacceptable level. A more permanent solution was needed to ensure that predators from a nearby area would not move in after the hunters left.

That solution came in the form of an innocuous-looking powder called strychnine, a toxin derived from the *nux vomica* bean, which grows in southern Asia and Australia. In its alkaloid form as a white crystalline powder, strychnine has a bitter taste, with even more bitter results. This fast-acting poison attacks the nervous system, causing extremely painful involuntary muscle contractions, even while the victim remains fully conscious. Because predators were often found dead within a few feet of poisoned bait, it was thought that strychnine was a quick and humane method of killing unwanted animals. However, observers watching poisoned bait recounted horror stories of the victims writhing and howling in pain for up to a half hour before they died.

Strychnine was so powerful that it had a domino effect, killing over and over again. The first animal that snatched so much as a single bite of a poisoned carcass quickly died, and any other animal or bird that fed on the dead predator also succumbed—until the predator base in the area of the bait was almost totally wiped out.

Strychnine also has lasting power. I unearthed this amazing story about the long-term effects of strychnine hidden deep in the archives section of the Missoula Country Library in Missoula, Montana. A rancher in the Powder River Country in eastern Montana employed an old trapper, called a wolfer, to rid his ranch of wolves and coyotes. The ranch was located not far from the Little Bighorn Battlefield. The wolfer placed beaver carcasses laced with strychnine along a series of gullies leading into the Powder River and quickly killed off the predators. As the wolfer was leaving, he warned the rancher to keep his dogs away from the area for a few years.

Five years later, the rancher came into possession of one of General George Armstrong Custer's prized greyhounds, truly one of the few survivors of the Little Bighorn massacre. One day the rancher rode into the river bottom with the greyhound. The dog trotted over to a bleached white beaver carcass and licked at it before returning to the rancher. Five minutes later the dog began whining and writhing on the ground. An hour later it was dead.

By the mid-1880s strychnine was stocked in most frontier mercantile stores, and there was an unwritten law that no cow man knowingly passed by a carcass without lacing it with a liberal dose of the stuff, in hopes of killing one or more wolves.

Although it was common knowledge among stockmen that the wolf was the main stock-killing culprit, the grizzly often took the brunt of the poison campaign. Between the years of 1885 and 1925, strychnine was probably responsible for more grizzly deaths than any other source. By the 1890s the grizzly was under siege everywhere. Its numbers had been greatly reduced in the river bottoms and across the plains, but the grizzly's mountain range was still relatively intact. As ranchers moved further into the foothills, those bears living in the hills occasionally came down to feast on a cow, dead or alive.

With the mind-set of those days being, "The only good bear is a dead bear," the newly formed U.S. Forest Service, whose job it was to protect wildlife in the mountains, instead sought to appease the influential community of ranchers, who were suspicious of government employees and the newly created national forest system. It was not unusual for forest service employees to take up trapping and poisoning predators both to cement relations with local ranchers and to collect the bounties offered. A ranger named Barker noted in his journal how he'd killed seven grizzlies in the Pecos National Forest in 1908.

Bowing to pressure from the western ranch lobby, the U.S. Congress created the Predatory Animal and Rodent Control (PARC) Division of the Department of Agriculture. With a healthy annual budget, PARC set in motion a strychnine-laced "final solution" to the predator problem. Government agents spread massive doses of the poison across the landscape. Hundreds of men were hired by PARC and issued a map and large gunnysacks bulging with fist-sized chunks of beef fat laced with strychnine. These "Johnny Appleseeds of death" spread out on horseback in a gridlike pattern across the West, throwing out lethal suet-balls as they went.

Wolf and grizzly numbers were decimated across the West by the long-lasting strychnine, and in many areas these two species ceased to exist. By 1917 only the White Mountains of Arizona held a few grizzlies, as did parts of the Mogollan Rim and Catalina-Rincon Mountains. A few grizzlies still inhabited the San Juan Mountains of northern New Mexico and southern Colorado, and the Abajo Mountains in southern Utah. In 1918 PARC tallies showed only twenty-eight grizzlies taken in New Mexico, and in 1920 only ten bears were killed in both New Mexico and Arizona.

Astonishingly, the poison campaign continued. PARC riders in 1924 spread more than 100,000 poison baits over cooperating ranches in New Mexico alone. The next year, 160,000 baits were spread over 75,000 square miles. Not only was PARC distributing poison and setting out bait stations on carcasses, but "approximately" 155,000 poison baits were given free of charge to cooperators in the predator war. In Colorado PARC men poisoned, shot, and trapped 5,148 bears. A total of 30 million acres were treated with strychnine throughout the West.

In 1928 the U.S. Forest Service estimated only about twenty-eight grizzlies in national forests in New Mexico, ten in Arizona, and two in Colorado. That year only one bear was killed by PARC. That year marked the beginning of the mop-up program to eliminate the last of the grizzlies. It was not unusual for a PARC hunter to waste up to two weeks to kill a lone grizzly hiding in some backcountry arroyo or mountain.

And then the U.S. Biological Survey Department dropped a bombshell. An official press release stated, "We find that very few bears are stock killers, and this department will begin doing all that is possible to discourage the killing of them. Only bears that are known stock killers are to be taken." The new administrator of PARC also publicly stated that the agency would use strychnine only in country where sheep were pastured, and where it was not possible to stop severe losses of livestock.

The reason for this sudden change in official attitude toward the grizzly came from the Eastern lobby, where the embryonic naturalist movement had begun. The U.S. Forest Service was responsible for the well-being of all lands and wild animal resources on federal land, and that included the grizzly bear. In addition there arose a general uproar among residents, even some stockmen, about PARC's continued use of poison drop baits, which killed family pets and even some livestock.

In an effort to staunch the killing of bears, the 1928 Arizona Legislature passed a provision that all bears were to be protected as game animals, with a hunting season from October 16 to November 30. But old habits and hatreds persisted. Government and private trappers, along with local residents seeking to ease the tedium of western life, were drawn to the excitement of a grizzly hunt. And with strychnine still available in mercantile stores, it was simply too tempting to not scatter some poison on a carcass. Newspapers often carried accounts of "the last grizzly" killed by some proud rancher or hunter.

THE NORTHERN GRIZZLY

Though strychnine was not used as liberally in the Northern Rockies and bordering states as it was farther south, sheep and cattle ranchers used it extensively in parts of the south and central portions of Idaho. Some ranchers in eastern Montana counties also used poison, often to kill off wolves, but if any wandering grizzlies also fell victim to it, so much the better.

PARC also penetrated Wyoming's seemingly vast wilderness and, with the help of strychnine-laced beef suet balls, managed to exterminate the great bear from all but the northwest corner of that state bordering Yellowstone National Park. Surplus bears that filtered down from the park were killed on sight. Colonel William Pickett, a Civil War veteran, founded a ranch on the Greybull River near present-day Meeteetsie, Wyoming, where he killed scores of grizzlies from 1877 to 1904. One fall Pickett killed 19 grizzlies over carcasses he'd set out. And just south of Yellowstone Park in Cody, Wyoming, lived Ned Frost, a famous hunter and guide who claimed he was involved in 350 bear killings.

In many areas strychnine was used in response to particular acts of predation, especially if the source of the problem was not quickly or easily eliminated. President Teddy Roosevelt recorded one such incident that occurred in 1888 near his ranch in Medora, South Dakota. A large grizzly bear, well known to locals by its tracks, was holed up in dense brushy bottom land along the Little Missouri River. The bear had acquired a taste for beef after feeding on a dead cow it found along the river.

THE GREAT BEAR ERADICATION

Roosevelt went along on a few hunts for the bear and mentioned that the bruin had taken to lying in wait along cattle trails and killing the first cow passing by, regardless of its size. Some of the ranchers, angered by their losses, hunted the bear extensively but were unsuccessful due to the dense tangles of willow along the river. Finally, a rancher sprinkled strychnine on a freshly killed cow carcass and killed the bear.

With the human populations in Washington and Oregon expanding rapidly, those states quickly eliminated the grizzly from within their borders. Only Montana, with its vast Rocky Mountain wilderness areas, held a small, verified population. Problem grizzlies were dealt with quickly, usually using traps, and it didn't take much for a rancher to call for government help.

During my interview with Bud Cheff, who lived among Native Americans in western Montana in the 1920s and spent most of his life around grizzlies, he recalled a neighbor who asked him to come over and trap a marauding grizzly that had killed several valuable draft horses. Cheff told me:

> There were four huge horses lying dead under a big Ponderosa pine tree. It was obvious to me that they'd taken shelter under the tree during a thunderstorm the night before and had been struck by lightning, but the farmer was in quite a state and got mad when I refused to set out my bear trap. He got a government trapper to come out and the guy set five big bear traps around the carcasses. It was summer and the bloated horses drew grizzlies down from the hills. That trapper killed more than a dozen grizzlies and black bears over the next month. It was one of the most irresponsible acts, by the rancher and the trapper, that I have ever seen committed against bears.

THE GREAT BEAR ERADICATION

EXTERMINATION OF THE GRIZZLY

Throughout the Southwest, California, the Central Rockies, and most of the Northern Rockies, not one stockman stepped forward to protect the grizzlies on his ranch. Not one U.S. Forest Service ranger took action to halt the bloodbath in his national forest. No influential landowner, attorney, or county or state official spoke out against eradicating the great bear. These men and their lands, in turn, received their due recompense. The grizzly vanished from their lands.

Texas was the first state to officially claim the extinction of the species within its borders when the last bear was killed there in 1890, followed by South Dakota in 1897. The official extinction date for the grizzly in Mexico was 1920. California, once the bastion of the giant grizzly bear, saw its last individual killed in 1922. Utah followed with the last grizzly killed in 1923. The last grizzly was killed in Oregon in 1931, in Washington in 1936, New Mexico in 1933, and Arizona in 1935.

The extermination of the grizzly caused few tears nationally. While the press lamented the slaughter of the buffalo—and the beaver before it and the elk after it—little ink was wasted on the demise of the great bear. And when a bear story appeared in the newspaper it was usually an account of the killing of a "last grizzly."

THE GRIZZLY REMNANT

By 1930 distraught conservationists declared the grizzly virtually extinct in the West, except for those few enclaves in the national parks of Yellowstone and Glacier, where the bear was protected. With stunning speed and efficiency, the grizzly had been eliminated. Or had it?

An article in the April 17, 1931, edition of the *Silver City* (New Mexico) *Enterprise* newspaper read: "To Carl and Blue Rice of Cliff goes the credit for killing one of the largest grizzly bears even seen in this section. They were riding their range and came upon a dead cow on

Rain Creek, and finding the tracks of a big grizzly bear around the carcass, they went to the nearest phone and called Supervisor James A. Scott and asked him to secure a permit to kill a bear out of season."

This bear was hailed as the last of the grizzlies in New Mexico. Problem was, a bear killed the year before on Black Mountain west of Magdalen by a man named George Evans had also been hailed as the last grizzly. Then in 1933 another "last grizzly" was killed in New Mexico—all in a state where the grizzly was "virtually" extinct.

Neighboring Arizona was also having problems with its "virtual extinction" of the great bear. An official "last grizzly" was killed on September 13, 1935, when Richard Miller shot a 300-pound bear near Red Mountain, located northeast of Clifton. But the next year, three experienced hunters encountered a grizzly in the same area. Then in 1939 a big grizzly was killed on the slopes of Mount Baldy. This bear has remained the official "last grizzly" in Arizona.

Sightings of silver-tipped bears persisted through the 1940s, along with rumors of a bear killed here and there, mostly by sheep men who had inundated many of those isolated corners in the West. Every sheep-herder carried a rifle to shoot on sight any coyote, mountain lion, or wolf. Or grizzly. Most certainly an unknown toll of "last grizzlies" were killed by sheep tenders who simply kept tight-lipped about it.

By 1950 even the most optimistic conservationists had thrown up their hands and removed the "virtual" from in front of "extinction." Those few scattered bears that might have somehow escaped the bullets, traps, hounds, or poison would have surely died off by then.

But they hadn't. And no area of the Southwest was more rife with grizzly bear rumors than the rugged San Juan Mountains in Southern Colorado. Those rumors became reality in September 1951. A federal trapper named Ernie Wilkinson was using poison to kill coyotes in the southern San Juan Mountains near Pagosa Springs after local sheep herders complained of predator problems. Wilkinson was using cyanide set-guns, called "getters," because of their flawless efficiency. A getter consists of a short tube with a firing apparatus at one end that employs a blank .22 rifle cartridge. The getter is buried in the ground until just the open end of the tube is visible. A cyanide pellet is dropped into the tube, then a fist-sized chunk of meat is forced over the open end and the gun is cocked. When an animal pulls on the bait, the gun fires the cyanide pellet into its mouth, killing it quickly. One morning when Wilkinson checked his set-guns he was stunned to find a young male grizzly lying dead a short distance from one of his getters.

Then it was learned that another small grizzly had been killed by a sheepherder 80 miles to the south. And in September of 1952, a third grizzly, this one a sow with two cubs, was killed following complaints that she had been killing sheep. This was the last official grizzly bear killed in the state of Colorado.

But in 1958 reports of yet another grizzly encounter surfaced 100 miles to the south, just across the New Mexico border. That summer Dr. Douglas Jester, a professor at New Mexico State University in Las Cruces, reported that he had several times observed a silver-tipped grizzly rummaging through a garbage dump beside black bears near Lake Malloy, west of the town of Raton. Though this bear was seen eighteen different times, wildlife officials in both Colorado and New Mexico never bothered to investigate. Ultimately the bear was killed by a Colorado game warden.

Talk persisted through the next two decades that grizzlies still roamed Colorado's rugged San Juan Mountains, but after twenty years of little more than rumors, even the most diehard grizzly enthusiast had to admit that this last bastion in the Southwest had seen the last of the great bear.

But that all changed again on the morning of September 23, 1979, when a local outfitter named Ed Wiseman was leading a bowhunting client down a narrow ridge in the South San Juan Mountains. Hoping to surprise a rutting bull elk, both men were quietly padding down a trail when the hunter spotted a large brown bear curled up asleep just ahead. Wiseman and his client circled the sleeping bear, but as they continued along the trail, the bear burst out of the brush. Wiseman tried to use his bow to fend off the animal and was knocked flat. The bear tore at Wiseman's leg, then grabbed his shoulder and shook him. Wiseman grabbed an arrow from his bow's quiver and jabbed the bear in the neck and ribcage. To Wiseman's amazement, the bear left him and walked a short distance before lying down. In a few minutes it was dead.

Contrary to what Colorado wildlife officials had been claiming for almost thirty years, the grizzly bear somehow continued to survive in the vast and rugged San Juan Mountains. State wildlife officials corrected themselves, admitting they'd been wrong. There had indeed been one last grizzly bear left—but it was now dead. There were no more.

Forensics proved wrong even that tongue-in-cheek hypothesis. The dead grizzly, a twenty-three-year-old female, had given birth; considering her age, she could have produced anywhere from two to twenty offspring. Where were they? And where were the adult males that had mated her?

The Ed Wiseman incident caused a public outcry by pro-grizzly conservationists and forced the state to send a crew into the South San Juans for two summers. Investigators found concrete evidence: Some hair samples tested positive as grizzly. Even this was looked upon with suspicion. Some skeptics wondered if the hairs had been planted by eco-fanatic bear enthusiasts, such as Doug Peacock, who at that time was leading his own grizzly search party in the San Juans. The chore of finding positive evidence of grizzly bears was made doubly difficult by the state's insistence that only very specific evidence would be accepted, such as a carcass, a track positively identified as a grizzly paw print by a recognized bear expert, a photograph by an expert, or DNA evidence from cells taken from an animal by a state official.

David Petersen, whose excellent book *Ghost Grizzlies: Does the Great Bear Still Haunt Colorado?* detailed numerous pieces of evidence to support the existence of grizzlies in the San Juans, was prepared to lead an expedition to find irrefutable evidence. But Petersen has since changed his mind. "There's such a circus atmosphere about the whole thing," he told me during a phone conversation. "If we find grizzlies in the San Juans, the place will be overrun with biologists trapping the bears, radio collaring them and further harassing them. My opinion now is to leave the last few grizzlies alone to live out their lives wild and free."

THE GREAT BEAR ERADICATION

Grizzly sightings continue in the San Juans. Petersen notes that in 1990 a female with three sub-adult cubs was observed from a distance of 80 yards with binoculars by local ranch foreman Dennis Schutz. "I've seen hundreds of bears," Schutz told Petersen, "and those were definitely grizzlies." Then in 1993 Petersen photographed a fresh bear dig in a remote subalpine bowl deep in the San Juans. (Grizzlies commonly excavate deep pits when digging for marmots.) In 1995 a large adult bear bluff-charged a hiker in the same area.

The Southwest was not the only region to go without any kind of organized response by wildlife agencies. In Southern Utah, instead of conserving a last foothold of the grizzly in the Paunsaugant area, state wildlife officials allowed sheep herders to flood the area. The usual sheep/bear problems ensued and the last of the grizzlies disappeared from that state.

My involvement with remnant populations of grizzlies began in 1970, when I joined the U.S. Forest Service. I was stationed at Red Ives, a remote, end-of-the-road ranger station in north Idaho's St. Joe National Forest. Our cook's husband, Lester Smith, was an old-time logger who entertained many of us young, wide-eyed forest-service workers with stories about the old days. I'd always been interested in wilderness animals such as wolves and grizzly bears. Within weeks of my arrival I discovered the official state position—that there were no wolves or grizzly bears in north Idaho—was erroneous when a large black wolf and a gray wolf trotted through our compound one morning.

Which led to another tantalizing question: *What about grizzlies?*

One evening I asked Smith if he'd ever seen a grizzly in northern Idaho. "I seen me a big grizzly back in the 1950s. Ol' Jack Horning and me were elk hunting up in the North Fork of the Coeur d'Alene River. We come around a corner on an old logging road and there the ol' boy stood, not more'n 30 yards away. Oh, he was a big brute!" Smith spread his arms wide to emphasize his point. "He was a perfect silvertip. He huffed and bounced stiff-legged at us and popped his teeth. Jack was gonna shoot him, but I told him not to. We just backed off and let that ol' bear wander into the brush."

When I asked why he'd let the bear escape, Smith shrugged and gave me his broken-toothed (the result of more than one hundred amateur boxing matches) grin and commented, "It's nice to know there's a few animals out there that ain't afraid of man."

Officially, the grizzly bear was said to be absent from all of Idaho except for a small portion of the Shoshone National Forest bordering the west side of Yellowstone National Park. Yet Lester Smith claimed to have encountered a grizzly barely a decade earlier.

That same year I met a man named Earl Law, an old trapper who still plied his historic trade along the St. Joe and St. Maries Rivers. When I asked him about grizzlies, he laughed and said:

> Oh yeah, me and my wife, May, had quite an experience one day when we were hiking along a trail in Canyon Creek [today, part of the Mallard-Larkins Roadless Area]. I think it was in 1952 or '53, somewhere around then. Anyway, we come around a corner and there's this big grizzly standing in the middle of the trail. It starts huffing and bellowing, and we dropped our backpacks in the middle of the trail and started backing up until we got to some big red fir trees and climbed them. The bear came bounding at us, but as soon as it got to the packs it stopped and started pawing at them. We watched it for probably ten minutes before it walked off the trail. I had a pistol with me, but I didn't want to shoot it. Seein' that grizzly was one of the highlights of my outdoor life.

In the eight years I spent in the upper St. Joe River country, a year didn't go by at the ranger station without a couple reports of grizzlies. One fall an elk hunter burst into the ranger station and announced that he'd shot and killed a small grizzly bear near St. Joe Lake, 6 miles up the river. Neither the forest service nor the state of Idaho bothered to send anyone to investigate. And why should they? Everyone knew there were no grizzlies in north Idaho.

But the rumors persisted, and I heard more grizzly stories as I interviewed other old timers. When I moved to Superior, Montana, which is just over the border from the St. Joe River country, I continued gathering grizzly stories. One of the most interesting accounts came from George Gildersleeve, an old, stoop-shouldered gold miner with a claim at the headwaters of Cedar Creek. Gildersleeve told me that sometime around 1960 a sheepherder rode into his mining camp and asked for help because something was killing his sheep. George agreed to investigate. At the time, the sheep were grazing at Hoodoo Meadows, located just across the state line in Montana. He recalled:

> I walked into this opening and there lies a dead sheep. And there's a big black bear layin' right next to it, but it's dead. I walked up to it, and its entire hindquarters were eaten, and something had pretty much pulverized its skull. Then I found these big, big bear tracks with long claw marks, and I knew it was a grizzly. I think that black bear had been killing those sheep, and the grizzly sneaked up and killed it. Boy, the hair raised up on the back of my neck as I stood there, knowing a grizzly was somewhere in the brush nearby, and I was molesting his food cache. All I had with me was a little 30-30 saddle carbine because I thought I'd be shooting at a coyote or a black bear. I eased away from that dead black bear and told the sheep herder to move his flock.

From my own research in the Northern Rockies and from verified sightings, killings, and other evidence farther south, it became obvious that a sustainable remnant population of grizzlies existed in isolated pockets from the Mexican Rockies up through the Southwest and into the Northern Rockies—at least through the 1950s, and in some areas into the 1970s.

But it was a tenuous existence, especially considering the grizzly's low reproductive rate. Females do not mate until they are four to five years old, and then only every two to three years after that. A low, scattered grizzly population runs the risk of failing to reproduce enough offspring to keep up with natural and human-caused bear mortality. Biologists claim that taking even one bear out of the system in some areas may doom the local grizzly population to extinction, with a minimum of six adult grizzlies (four of them females) necessary to sustain themselves. And a few more wouldn't hurt. A grizzly bear reintroduction plan for the Bitterroot Divide (see chapter 4) that separates Idaho and Montana calls for a total of twenty-five bears to be released during a five-year period.

Bear enthusiasts consider the slaughter of grizzlies in the early decades of the twentieth century a tragedy. But the events of the following decades must be considered in the same light, for there is incontrovertible evidence that a viable remnant population of grizzlies still survived. What the great bear desperately needed was a change in men's hearts and minds. Unfortunately, the stockman mentality—the idea of treating every grizzly as a killer—prevailed throughout the Southwest and into Mexico.

Even some of those men who would later be honored as great environmentalists remain suspect on the subject of protecting the grizzly. Aldo Leopold, considered by many as the father of wildlife conservation and whose 1949 book *A Sand County Almanac* has become required reading for environmentalists, at one time was in a position to help the great bear. Leopold was supervisor of New Mexico's Carson National Forest in 1912 when that federal land was overrun with 7,000 head of cattle, 200,000 sheep, and 400 homesteads. Small wonder the place had a predator problem! Under Leopold's leadership, wolves and grizzlies in that area of the South San Juan Mountains were decimated, not only by private hunters and trappers but also by forest service employees.

Leopold's *Escudillo* essay, which recounts the killing of a "last grizzly" on Escudillo Mountain in Arizona by a wandering government trapper, undoubtedly changed the hearts and minds of readers, but he was essentially preaching to the choir. What was needed from Leopold was not an elegant book of prose by a retired U.S. Forest Service official in his later years but a courageous effort by Leopold during his active years to stop the grizzly eradication.

I also recall an issue of *Defenders Magazine* (the flagship publication of the conservation group Defenders of Wildlife) that carried an expose by a prominent retired government trapper. This man related how he had destroyed thousands of coyotes, wolves, and bears in the American Southwest during a career that spanned the critical years from 1940 to 1970. In my view he remained silent until reaching retirement age, living on a comfortable pension wrought from the blood of wolves and bears, before admitting to his part in the slaughter.

Sadly, no one in the Southwest rose to the forefront to save the remnant of grizzlies that survived the great bear eradication. In fact the only positive views I have received concerning the grizzly bear have come from grizzled old men in the Northern Rockies. This quite possibly may come down to a simple matter of economics. Western Montana and Northeast Idaho, where the grizzly still had a precarious foothold in the 1940s and '50s, were less dependent on livestock than other parts of grizzly country. In fact, none of the three old-timers appearing in this chapter were ranchers or farmers. Lester Smith was a logger; Earl Law, a trapper; and George Gildersleeve, a gold miner.

One can only wonder what great environmental success stories might be shared today at bear conferences if someone such as young Aldo Leopold, or a group of federal land managers and trappers, had united to halt the killing of grizzlies in Colorado's San Juan Mountains, or in New Mexico and Arizona, or if the Craighead brothers had chosen the South San Juans, rather than Yellowstone, as their base of operations for informing the public about the plight of the grizzly.

Nonetheless, the Craigheads and the other men featured in the following chapters were instrumental in educating an American public largely ignorant of the majesty and fragility of *Ursus horribilis*. But so too were lesser-known men, such as Lester Smith, who through the years convinced hundreds of fresh-faced forest service workers to be more tolerant of the wild animals living beyond the glow of the smoky kerosene lantern in their bunkhouse.

CHAPTER 2

EARLY BEAR LOVERS

James Capen "Grizzly" Adams, William Wright, and Teddy Roosevelt loved bears. Problem is, they mostly loved them dead. Wright and Adams killed bears by the score—some blacks, but mostly grizzlies. Roosevelt accounted for several grizzlies even though he was terrifically busy commanding the Rough Riders in battle during the Spanish-American War and later leading the nation as its president. These men killed bears for monetary gain; they killed bears for sport; they killed bears for trophy rugs; and sometimes they killed bears just to kill them.

And yet, much of the credit for the existence of the grizzly in the lower states today must go to Adams, Wright, and Roosevelt. Their penned exploits, while admittedly brutal and at times bordering on the sadistic, most assuredly influenced many young men in succeeding generations to look beyond the killing of the grizzly and to seek instead the value and worth of the great bear as one of the most majestic, powerful creatures on the face of the earth—sentiments almost unheard of in the latter part of the nineteenth century.

The following accounts of their exploits should be read in the context of their times, when the country west of the Mississippi was still largely wilderness, and the general population of America was not yet enlightened toward the concept of wildlife conservation. Reading about the lives of Adams, Wright, and Roosevelt also provides us with a breathtaking window back in time to the days when the grizzly was shot on sight and reveals how difficult it must have been for any man to buck the socioeconomic trend of killing bears for fun or profit. It is also interesting to follow in their lives the slow metamorphosis from bear killer to bear lover.

JAMES CAPEN "GRIZZLY" ADAMS

James Capen Adams was born in Medway, Mississippi, and didn't arrive in California until the autumn of 1849 during the gold rush. Mining wasn't in his blood, though, so he turned to the one thing that did interest him: wild animals. Leaving behind the teeming cities and gold-mining towns, Adams headed for the mountains with a team of oxen pulling an old wagon, two rifles, and a pistol, along with several bowie knives.

Besides being an excellent shot, Adams possessed a variety of skills that served him well in the wilderness. He became an expert at constructing log cabin traps for bears and also made the steel cages to transport them back to civilization for bear/bull fights or for export. During his first trip afield, he killed several grizzlies, often administering the coup de grace with his bowie knife. Adams was soon doing a brisk trade in the export of pelts and wild animals, and it was his uncanny ability to bring back alive a large collection of lethal predators that furnished Adams with his first taste of notoriety and acclaim. A flurry of activity always surrounded Adams when, dressed in buckskins and beaver hat, he strolled triumphantly through San Francisco's wharf district on his way to the docks with a great menagerie of wild animals drawn behind him in wagons.

In the summer of 1853, while on a hunt in Eastern Washington Territory (probably present-day Montana), Adams killed a sow grizzly with two cubs. The men chased down and captured the orphaned young. Adams chained the female cub to a tree and muzzled her, then set about "training" her. After trying kindly advances without success,

Adams became incensed when the cub swatted his offered hand. He then proceeded to beat her relentlessly until she was reduced to an exhausted, whimpering ball of fur. When he reached out to touch her, she did not protest, instead trembling in fear. Soon he was stroking her lovingly and feeding her by hand. He named her Lady Washington. Before long the bear was allowed to roam around camp on a tether and eventually learned to follow Adams without a tether. On one of her first hunting trips with Adams, Lady Washington assisted him in routing a wild grizzly.

Amazingly, Lady Washington was also taught, after a series of beatings, to carry small packs on her back. The California Menagerie, as it came to be called, caused quite a stir that fall when Adams strolled through the streets of Portland, Oregon, leading every sort of wild animal imaginable, along with Lady Washington, now weighing 300 pounds, walking placidly beside him with a bundle of hides on her back. Much to his pleasure, he was referred to thereafter as "Grizzly" Adams.

In the early spring of 1854, Grizzly Adams and a Mr. Solon of Sonora traveled through Yosemite Valley and discovered a grizzly den. Adams shot the bear and heard whimpering inside. He crawled into the den and came out with two tiny cubs, sightless and probably only a week old. Adams named the cubs General Jackson and Ben Franklin. A greyhound in the party was nursing a litter of pups, so Adams had the grizzly cubs suckle on the dog.

Later that year, Adams took a trip east of the Sierra Nevada through Nevada and into Utah seeking wild animals to kill and trap. While he was camped in the mountains, Lady Washington was visited several nights by a Rocky Mountain grizzly. Though tempted to kill the interloper, Adams held off as long as Lady Washington showed no indication of leaving with the big male. His hunch paid off, for the next year Lady Washington gave birth to a single cub that Adams named Fremont.

Leaving mother and cub behind, Adams returned to the Sierra Nevada on a hunting trip. While he was passing through a chaparral thicket, a huge female grizzly with three cubs sprang upon Adams, knocked his gun away, and threw him to the ground. Ben Franklin attacked the female at the throat, causing the bigger bear to turn on him.

This gave Adams time to grab his rifle and kill the sow, but both Ben and Adams carried wicked scars of the fight for the rest of their lives.

Actually, the capture and domestication of grizzly cubs was not unheard of in those days. To capture and try to domesticate a full-grown grizzly, on the other hand, was considered suicidal. This dubious honor fell to Grizzly Adams in the winter of 1855.

Adams built a large log cabin trap along the Mercedes River in Northern California. Months after first baiting the trap, Adams was awakened in the middle of the night by the unearthly bellowing of a bear. With pine torches, Adams and two Indian boys approached the trap and found a huge grizzly "taking chips out of the pine logs faster than I could with an axe."

To distract the bear from tearing through the logs, Adams thrust a torch into its face, then prodded it back with sharp sticks and hot rods. Adams camped on top of the log cabin trap for eight days to keep the huge brute from escaping. He finally left the boys to watch over the bear and hastened for Stockton to fetch a steel cage.

It took weeks for Adams to return with the massive steel cage, and he found that the big grizzly had lost much of his weight, but not of his fight. When the cage was butted up to the door and the door opened, the grizzly refused to leave, and all the burning fire brands and red-hot pokers could not induce him further.

Adams was forced, at the risk of life and limb, to pass a heavy chain through the steel bars of the cage, then into the trap. After a day of trying, Adams finally got the chain around the bear's head. Then with the oxen pulling mightily on the chain and the men "burning, punching and pulling" finally forced the furiously battling bear into the steel cage. Only after Adams was assured that he'd be able to get the berserk grizzly out alive did he name the bear Samson, alluding to the strong man of biblical times.

Grizzly Adams had proven his bravery with wild animals, but even he knew his limits with Samson. He was eventually able to display the huge bear, but always with a heavy chain fastened around his neck. Regardless, visitors took one look at the menacing stare of the enormous bear and gave him a wide berth.

EARLY BEAR LOVERS

Anxious to show off his captured animals, Adams opened a live museum on Clay Street in San Francisco. He proved to be a natural showman and his sizeable menagerie of wild birds and animals began to draw large audiences nightly. Theodore Hittell, a young reporter for the *Daily Evening Edition* in San Francisco, wrote:

> Descending the stairway, I found a most remarkable spectacle. The basement was a large one but with a low ceiling, and dark, dingy in appearance. In the middle, chained to the floor, were two large grizzly bears, named Ben Franklin and Lady Washington. They paced restlessly in circles. Not far off were several other younger grizzlies and black bears also chained. Near the front of the room was an open stall in which were haltered several mature elks. Further back were cages with lions and several other California animals. At the rear, in a very large iron cage, was the monster grizzly, Samson. He was an immense creature weighing some three-quarters of a ton, and from his look and actions, as well as the care taken to rail him from the spectators, it was evidenced that he should not be approached too closely.

Amazed by the unprecedented display of wild animals and mesmerized by the life of the shaggy-haired, craggy-faced man called Grizzly Adams, Hittell recorded the loquacious mountain man's bizarre life story. Adams, always the showman, gladly accommodated Hittell, and many of his exploits appeared in newspaper and magazine articles in San Francisco and eventually in publications on the East Coast.

These written accounts of Grizzly Adams's adventures brought him much attention and drew hundreds of visitors to his San Francisco museum, mostly to see his big grizzlies. With a 50-cent admission rate, Adams should have become a rich man, but his talents lay in hunting and training bears, not in finances. The landlord sued him for $1,000 in back rent. Disgusted, Adams marched his entire menagerie onto a boat and sailed for New York, hopeful that the Eastern cities would be more appreciative of his menagerie.

GRIZZLY ADAMS
GETS A TELEVISION MAKEOVER

On February 1, 1977, NBC aired an hour-long nature-based adventure program titled "The Life and Times of Grizzly Adams." Starring Dan Haggerty as the famous James Capen "Grizzly" Adams, the first episode portrayed Adams as a gentle man seeking the solitude of wilderness who befriended an orphaned grizzly cub (Ben). Together this unlikely team of man and bear went about solving life's problems. Their most amazing accomplishment was the bridging of the language barrier. When Haggerty spoke to Ben, this amazing bear somehow understood him and responded with head wags and nods, or occasional bawls and grunts.

The series was long on sentiment and short on historical accuracy, for the real Grizzly Adams did things a bit differently. Desiring a young grizzly to train, Adams located a den, stuck his gun barrel against the groggy mother's head, and blew her brains out, at which point he yanked two bawling cubs out of the hole and proceeded to "train" them. The real Grizzly Adams accomplished his training by using clubs, chains, and whips to beat the young bears into quivering balls of submission. Eventually, one cub, which he later called Lady Washington, was successfully trained. Nothing more is heard about the other cub. It may have died from the beatings, or Adams deemed it "untrainable" and sent it to join its mother in oblivion. But then, television has never felt any particular obligation toward historical accuracy.

When the grizzly appeared in early-day films, it was usually a murderous beast to be hunted down and killed for the safety of mankind. But that all changed when Sunn Classics Pictures released "Grizzly Adams" as a feature film in 1974. The movie told the tale of a man who lived and communicated with the mighty grizzly. It struck a chord in the hearts of an increasingly conservation-minded urban American public, and the $140,000 film grossed more than $65 million at the box office.

The film had been the brainchild of Charles E. Sellier, who then began surveying national audiences and became convinced that a prime-time television program about Grizzly Adams was exactly what American audiences wanted to see. And deferring to the whims of this test audience, who had heavy leanings toward PETA, Dan Haggerty wore no animal skins and ate no meat. In fact, the test audiences even nixed the idea of Haggerty becoming involved with a woman because they wanted to keep his character pure and always ready to seek the peace and harmony of nature without some messy relationship clogging his mellow brain waves.

"The Life and Times of Grizzly Adams" ran for two seasons, 1977–1978. However, syndicated reruns and videos of favorite programs are still being viewed by audiences today. Without a doubt, this program was a catalyst for a great many nature programs to come— shows that depicted wild animals in a favorable light and man as the evil interloper.

When Adams stepped ashore, the great circus owner P.T. Barnum was waiting. The two men immediately hit it off, and Barnum signed the Grizzly Adams Menagerie to a series of exhibits. In 1860 Barnum wrote:

> This man [Adams] was eminently what is called a "character," there being a bravery enough and romantic in his nature to make him a real hero. From his many years in the Sierras and Rockies, he developed recklessness to his character, which added to his air of invincibility, rendering him one of the most striking men for his age.
>
> His menagerie of California animals, captured in the wilds by himself, consisted of twenty or thirty immense grizzly bears, at the head of which was old Samson. Old Adams trained these monsters so that with him they were docile as kittens, though in fact many of the most ferocious among them would attack a stranger without hesitation. In fact, the training of these animals was no fool's play, as old Adams learned at his cost, for the terrific blows, which he received from time to time, while teaching them docility, will ultimately cost him his life.

Barnum went on to explain his prophetic statement about Adams's demise:

> He met with me upon his arrival in New York. He was dressed in his hunter suit of buckskin trimmed with furs and borders of dangling tails of animals he had trapped in the wilds. His cap was the skin of a wolf's head and shoulders, from which dangled several more small animal tails. In fact, old Adams was quite as much a show as his wild animals.
>
> During our meeting, Adams mentioned that his bears were getting the best of him and took off his cap and showed me the top of his head. His skull was literally broken in. It had on various occasions been struck by the fearful paws of his grizzly students; and the last blow, from the bear called General Fremont, had lain open his

brain so that its workings were plainly visible. I remarked that such a dangerous wound might prove fatal.

Adams shrugged and replied, "Yes, that will fix me out. It had nearly healed, but old Fremont opened it for me for the third or fourth time before I left California, and he did his business so thoroughly that I am a used up man. However, I reckon I may live another six months or a year yet." This was spoken as cooly as if he had been talking about the life of a dog.

On the morning of the show's opening, a band accompanied Grizzly Adams's parade of his menagerie down Broadway and up the Bowery. As expected, even with all the wild animals, Adams stole the show, dressed in his outrageous hunting costume at the head of the parade in a large wagon. Three immense grizzlies were in the wagon, with the grizzly bear man holding them with only a single chain in his hands. All the while he was seated atop the back of the biggest of the bears.

This bear was the famous General Fremont and with Adams was as docile as a kitten. But as docile as these animals were, there was not one among them that would not occasionally give Adams a sly blow or bite when a good chance was offered; hence Adams was but a terrible physical wreck of his former self and expressed pretty much the truth when he said:

> Mr. Barnum, I am not the man I was five years ago. . . . I have been beaten to jelly, torn almost limb from limb, and nearly chawed up and spit out by these treacherous grizzly bears. However, I am good for a few months yet, and I hope we shall gain enough money to make my old woman comfortable, for I have been absent from her for some years.

Doctors who examined Adams gave him but a few weeks to live and suggested he be hospitalized. But Grizzly Adams refused and, though in excruciating pain, gritted his teeth and delivered performance after performance to fulfill his six-month contract. As soon as he was finished, he dragged his feverish, broken body to bed and never got up from it.

EARLY BEAR LOVERS

Theodore Hittell's book *The Adventures of James Capen Adams, Mountaineer and Grizzly Bear Hunter of California* came out in the summer of 1860, while Adams was bed-ridden. It was an instant success among the adventure-hungry eastern establishment and would surely have catapulted Grizzly Adams to celebrity status, but he died just a few months after the book's publication.

Many of Grizzly Adams's hunting techniques, especially the deplorable practice of seeking out sow grizzlies and killing them to capture their young, were shrugged off by a public calloused to the hardships of wild animals, especially the fearsome grizzly bears. However, when these bears grew up and appeared before thousands of people, it cast the grizzly bear in a far better light—powerful and potentially lethal, but also a magnificent beast to be respected and, yes, even admired. Many young men around the turn of the century read the book and were struck not only by the courage and fearlessness of Grizzly Adams but also by the magnificence of the great bear. Every person I interviewed for this book had read the Grizzly Adams book. Howard Copenhaver told me that after he read the book, he jumped on his horse and went looking for a grizzly in the Bob Marshall Wilderness. Not to hunt or kill one; he just wanted to sit down and look at it.

Unfortunately, Grizzly Adams could not save himself from the grizzlies he loved, nor could he save them from other men. As mentioned earlier, old habits die hard, and change often comes slowly. The California grizzly became extinct in 1922, and one must wonder how Adams would have felt about losing his friends who, like himself, asked no quarter and gave none.

WILLIAM WRIGHT

William Wright was born in 1856 on a hardscrabble farm in New Hampshire, where the drudgery of work was a constant. After dinner the family would gather around the woodstove and listen to his father read. One evening, William's dad began to read from a book titled *The*

EARLY BEAR LOVERS

Adventures of James Capen Adams, Mountaineer and Grizzly Bear Hunter of California. William and his brother pestered their father to read the book over and over again; and though the boys could not yet read, they virtually wore out the book while studying its sketches and illustrations.

When William was about six years old, the P.T. Barnum Circus came to town, and in its menagerie was one of the bears that Grizzly Adams had captured. William Wright reminisced years later in his book *The Grizzly Bear,* "That bear was the only thing I can recall from that circus. I went back every few minutes to look at him; and I can see in my mind even now the way he paced back and forth. I dreamed, boy-like, of emulating Adams, and I openly declared my resolve. Strangely, I never changed my mind even as I grew older." Through his formative years, Wright maintained his desire to someday seek out the wild grizzly. Though his apprenticeship as a blacksmith and a machinist almost took him to Australia, Wright at the last minute switched plans and took a train west, hopping off in Spokane, Washington. William Wright, at long last, had arrived in grizzly country.

But the fledgling grizzly-bear hunter had a lot to learn. Unfortunately, he listened to and believed much of the misinformation about the great grizzled bear that still stalked some of the forests around Spokane. The most prevalent myth was that one needed only walk to the head of a draw and allow his scent to blow down it. Any grizzly bear, upon catching a whiff of human in the area, would make straight for that man with the intention of attacking him. Wright quickly discovered that not only was this information false, the opposite was true. The grizzly strove mightily to go the other way, rather than face a man with a gun.

After moving to Missoula, Montana, Wright began roaming the wild Bitterroot Mountains that separate Idaho from Montana. On the Idaho side he came upon a cascading, boulder-strewn stream teeming with spawning salmon, and there in the mud were fresh bear tracks. Wright wrote:

> As I waited along the stream, I was not uncomfortable at
> first, but as the sun dipped behind the ridge, I began to

41

tremble but still did not want to give up the hunt. Then my teeth began to chatter and I decided that I would wait five more minutes and then leave.

When I stood to leave, I looked upstream and saw a grizzly very much like the old bear I had studied in the circus cage many years before. The brute was headed straight for me. I hunkered down and waited until he was so close that escape would be impossible. As I raised my rifle, it seemed certain that my dream of a lifetime was to come true. When some forty yards off, he turned a little to go around a bush and presented a perfect shot. I raised up, aimed carefully just on the point of the shoulder close to the neck, and pulled the trigger.

It never entered my thoughts but that the bear would drop in its tracks. One can, therefore, imagine my surprise when he gave a roar like a mad bull and came my way on the jump. My rifle jammed . . . it looked like I would shortly have all the grizzly down on me I ever wanted. Terrified, I dropped my gun and dove over the stream bank and hid under it. The water was ice cold and I was almost frozen before I jumped in, but now had no regrets. After a half hour of no grizzly charging over the bank after me, I eased out of the water and, though terrified, eased my way toward my rifle. When I finally got a fresh load in it, I again felt brave and began to search for the bear. To my amazement, the brute had expired no more than twenty yards from where he had been shot.

The old grizzly was everything Wright had ever wanted, but he soon found that the Lochsa River was not only full of salmon, it was also full of bears. William Wright, true to his word, loved bears. He loved them to death. Like a man possessed, he embarked on an orgy of unrestrained killing.

A short time after his first Idaho bear kill, Wright discovered winding along the river a major bear trail that held a 14-inch-long track. He became obsessed with finding the big bear responsible for that track. One evening after a fresh rain, he sneaked forward with gun in hand and murder on his mind:

As luck would have it, when I reached the fir trees and took a look at the hillside. There sat an old grizzly about a hundred yards above the brink of the canyon and three hundred yards from me. I immediately began the sneak of my life. I got down on the ground and sneaked through the tangle of brush.

I dared to take a peek at the bear I was after, but when I looked about, I spied another bear further down in the canyon. This was the largest bear I had ever seen in my life and surely was the one who had made those huge tracks. This was the bear I had wanted all my life.

I set my precedence on this big bear, but yet I wanted both bears. I held off shooting until the big bear had moved within a hundred yards of the other bear. I crept to the top of a small ridge and was rewarded with the sight of the big bear forty yards below me, and the other bear at sixty yards.

I took a sitting position that afforded me a good shot at both bears. And with one cartridge in the gun, I placed three others on the ground, and held two more in the hand that held the gun up. I waited until I had a perfect shot at the big bear. When I shot, the brute immediately slumped to the ground while I ejected the spent shell and rammed another cartridge into the chamber. While the second bear stood erect, wondering what had happened; I put a bullet through his chest and dropped him also. What an accomplishment to have killed two immense grizzly bears with two shots just seconds apart. But my good fortune was not yet over.

I heard scrambling from another ravine to my left, and when I look, I saw a big sow grizzly leading two cubs up the ravine. I waited until the sow reached the top and then shot her. She rolled back into the ravine and, of course, this stopped her two cubs, and they fell to my next two shots. I was wet from head to toe and covered with mud and dirt, but it was well worth it. Five grizzlies down in as many shots and minutes. This was the greatest bag of grizzlies I ever made single-handed.

Wright continued killing grizzlies with regularity, but something was happening inside him. Though painfully (for the grizzlies) slow in coming, there began to appear cracks in his facade as the great hunter and killer of grizzlies. He noted:

One time I watched as four grizzlies caught salmon in a riffle. I sat open-mouthed watching them swat salmon clear out of the water onto the bank. One of the bears disappeared into the brush after its fish, but I wanted to kill the three remaining bears before they left.

I presume that, as I looked at the three remaining bears, I was the victim of what nowadays would be called a game-hog, for I desired to kill all three. I was a little upstream from them and fifty yards away. I fired at the smallest bear, and it dropped into a deep pool. The other bear started to leave, but I shot it a little farther back and it bounded for shore. When I then turned my attention to the third bear, all I saw was the rustle of bushes where it had disappeared.

But now that the excitement was over, my excitement was short-lived. The hides were not worth taking off. It had been a useless slaughter and I was sorry that I had killed. I took the large teeth and long claws of the dead bears, but since then I have never, but once, shot a grizzly when it was fishing.

Wright's bloodlust may have been satiated, but his responsibility for the killings of numerous grizzlies continued when he became an outfitter. One time he led a man from New York whose life's dream was to kill a mighty grizzly. While the men were hiking back to camp at dusk, they surprised a big grizzly beside a massive logjam. Wright recalled:

It was dark enough that the man could not shoot, but when the big bear hopped onto the stream bank above, he was silhouetted against the sky and I risked a shot. The bear snorted and barreled through the brush. Being too dark to take up the blood trail we went back to camp and waited for the morning.

It rained heavily overnight, washing out the blood trail. Having taken a risky shot, we both agreed that the shot may even have been a miss, though we eventually found some blood under a large spruce tree where the rain had not washed it away. Three days later our cook spotted several buzzards circling about and swooping down the mountain, and we went over to investigate. He found, between two large boulders that were nearly overgrown with brush, the body of the old bear. He had crawled in between the rocks and had covered the entrance so completely that we passed by it twice and never saw it. The hide was quite useless. We took the teeth and claws of the poor old fellow, but I would gladly have returned them to him with his life, if I could have. ·

Unfortunately, Wright did not stop hunting at that point. Instead he changed location, moving north to the Selkirk Mountains of British Columbia, where he continued hunting grizzlies. Then it was back to Idaho's Clearwater River country north of the Lochsa. Several times he encountered grizzly sows with cubs, and during the excitement and bloodlust of the hunt, the sow was killed and the cubs dispatched, if for no other reason than to cease their pitiful bawling over their fallen mother.

In Wright's memoir it becomes apparent that the senseless murders of these baby bears began to eat at him. The massive, gluttonous blood drenching that he had at one time gleefully recounted eventually began to wear on his mind. The memories of baby bears bawling for their dead mothers inspired a fairly momentous decision. William Wright, who claims to have killed more than fifty grizzlies, put down his gun and began to approach the grizzly bear in a far different—and more humane—way.

He wrote:

> In the beginning I studied the grizzly in order to hunt him. For many years I pitted my shrewdness against his, and my endurance against his, and many a time I came out the winner, and many a time I came out the loser.
>
> And then at last my interest in my opponent grew to overshadow my interest in the game [of killing the grizzly]. I came to hunt him in order to study him. I LAID MY RIFLE ASIDE . . . it has been twelve years since I killed my last grizzly. Yet in all those years there is not one that I have not spent at least some time in grizzly country. For then [alas! I regret that it had not been sooner] I undertook to hunt him instead with a camera.

In 1906 Wright undertook the Herculean task of photographing a grizzly using a cumbersome, forty-pound wooden camera that produced 8-by-10 negatives and employed the dangerous phosphorus powder for a flash. Wright noted with sadness, "I must travel to Yellowstone because the wonderful Clearwater River country has seen the demise of the grizzly there."

His experiences in Yellowstone, especially with bears that came to dumps, were illuminating in light of the tremendous controversy that would erupt a half-century later between the Craighead brothers and the National Park Service over the closing of these dumps. Essentially, Wright observed, "When the grizzlies were a hundred yards from the dump site, they became once again as wild as any grizzly I have ever seen."

Like Grizzly Adams, Wright's experiences resulted in a book, *The Grizzly Bear,* which he wrote in 1906. Wright's memoir appealed to a nation of young men in the early decades of the twentieth century who yearned for adventure and the outdoor life. Several grizzled old men whom I interviewed mentioned Wright's book as a document that made them rethink their opinions on the great bear. Wright courageously admitted in his book that in thought and deed, he had been wrong: He had been a game hog and a butcher, and he'd killed and helped extirpate an animal more worthy of his respect than his bullets.

The Grizzly Bear ends with a plea to men of courage to arm themselves, not with powder and ball but rather with a fearless determination to see the great bear as a national treasure instead of as a trophy:

> Later, as the years passed and I became less enamored of killing, I have been interested in the study of these animals, one and all . . . But not only as a sportsman did my interest in the grizzly survive the discovery that all my early romantic ideas about him were ill-founded, but as a student, I have steadily added to my admiration for him.
>
> He is the one wild animal of the wilderness that owns no natural overlord. With the exception of man he deigns to recognize no enemy. And if he is not, as he once was thought, the bloodthirsty and tyrannous autocrat of his vast domain, he is none the less the master. If, in sober truth, he is less terrible than he was painted, he only loses interest and dignity in the eyes of those whom fear alone impresses.
>
> In short, just as the grizzly was in the beginning the lure that drew me to the wilderness, so in my mind, he remains the grandest animal our country knows.

TEDDY ROOSEVELT

Theodore Roosevelt may have been born with a silver spoon in his mouth, but there was no silver lining in his lungs. The first son of affluent New Yorkers, Teedie, as he was called as a child, suffered from acute asthma. During those precarious days of Teedie's early life, if anyone had predicted the boy would one day become an impressive physical specimen, a fearless adventurer and outdoorsman, the father of modern conservation, and one of the most popular presidents of the United States, Mr. Roosevelt would have laughed them to scorn. A more realistic goal at that time would have been to see his son live through the night.

But live he did, though for several years Teedie was confined to life indoors, where he usually gravitated to his father's library, which contained all the classic books of the literary world, plus an ample assortment of adventure novels and books by famous explorers. Roosevelt during this time most likely read *The Journals of Lewis & Clark* and John Hittell's biography of Grizzly Adams.

As he grew older, Teedie's severe asthma miraculously abated, and he began to venture outdoors more and more until, by the age of ten, he was spending every daylight hour exploring the nearby forests and streams. Much to his mother's dismay, Teedie often brought bugs, spiders, mice, rats, snakes, and other objectionable "specimens" into the Roosevelt house.

But even as a strapping youth, Teddy Roosevelt still suffered from one lingering physical ailment—poor eyesight. He often suffered intense headache from eyestrain. Even more serious was the fact that the double-barreled shotgun his father had given him to collect specimens was of little use because he couldn't see well enough to shoot. After a visit to an optometrist, a spectacled Teddy Roosevelt walked out of that office with his eyes wide open for the first time in his life. As soon as he arrived home, he grabbed his shotgun and headed for the woods to collect "specimens," an endeavor that would last a lifetime.

During his freshman year at Harvard, Roosevelt studied to be a naturalist, but much to his dismay, he discovered that naturalists spent most of their time in dimly lit laboratories studying the minutest properties of specimens. Teddy wanted action, so he changed his focus to law and gained a degree in that field.

Roosevelt began to delve into politics, first as a New York state assemblyman. Wealthy and now politically connected, and with a beautiful wife and a baby on the way, Roosevelt, it appeared, had it all. But dark clouds loomed ahead.

Within twenty-four hours Roosevelt lost his wife during child-birth, and then his mother passed away. Near mad with grief and anger, he headed west, with no intention of ever returning to New York. He had been to the Dakota Territory the previous year and had harvested a buffalo. He'd been mesmerized by the invigorating life in the still wild West, and this time when he arrived at Medora, Dakota Territory, he purchased a ranch and 450 head of cattle. The cattle business and the cowboys who tended the herds were a rough and tumble lot, but the irrepressible Roosevelt readily took to the harshness and adventure of everyday life: roping steers, branding, even tracking down three horse thieves and returning them at gunpoint to the sheriff.

The nightlife in the bawdy cowboy saloons of Medora was just as rough, and fistfights, even shootouts, were not uncommon. A perceived weakness was an invitation for trouble. Roosevelt's eyeglasses were looked upon by a few of the cowboys as an unmanly adornment. One night a cowboy made a smirking "four eyes" remark, whereupon Roosevelt called him out to fight. The man backed down, but the next night a town bully, wielding two pistols, berated the bespectacled Roosevelt, calling him "storm windows" and "four eyes." Before the troublemaker could even raise a hand, Roosevelt delivered a tremendous punch to the man's jaw and knocked him out cold.

Leaving dependable hired hands to tend to his cattle, Roosevelt pursued one of his favorite pastimes—hunting. He killed several elk, antelope, mule deer, and black bears, but fell short of his goal of a grizzly bear. With great determination he set off for the Bighorn Mountains in what is now Wyoming on a grizzly hunt with his ranch foreman, Bill Merrifield.

Roosevelt killed a large bull elk one late afternoon, and while he was hiking out in the dwindling light of dusk, he made a disturbing discovery. He later wrote: "I came across the huge, half-human footprints of a great grizzly, which must have passed by within minutes. It gave me an eerie feeling in the silent, lonely woods, to see for the first time the unmistakable proofs that I was in the home of the lord of the wilderness."

When Roosevelt returned the next day with Merrifield, they discovered that the bear had been feeding on the elk carcass. They waited in ambush all day, but the animal didn't appear. After sunset, as they were preparing to leave, they heard branches snapping in the nearby forest. The grizzly was coming to the carcass. Unfortunately, it was dark before the bear began pulling and tearing at the dead elk, and Roosevelt dared not risk a shot.

The next morning, Merrifield, a good tracker, took up the bear's tracks. The men followed the bear into a dark forest littered with downed trees. As Merrifield passed by a huge pine log, he dropped to one knee. Roosevelt eased forward with rifle raised. Suddenly, the huge grizzly stood up, and Roosevelt took steady aim at the bear's head and pulled the trigger. The bear dropped in its tracks. Roosevelt estimated the grizzly's weight at over 1,000 pounds and later claimed it was the biggest grizzly bear he ever killed or saw, dead or alive.

Though Roosevelt was very pleased with his first grizzly, Merrifield was frankly disappointed because the great bear had not lived up to its ferocious reputation. Two days later, the men came upon another grizzly, and since Merrifield had not yet killed one, Roosevelt gave him the nod. However, Merrifield paused, and then whispered in Roosevelt's ear, "I'll break his leg, and we'll see what he'll do." Roosevelt later wrote that he imposed a rather emphatic veto, whereupon the disappointed Merrifield dropped the bear with a shot to the shoulder.

Merrifield got his wish a few days later when they chased down an old sow grizzly with a nearly grown cub. Both men wounded the sow as she escaped into a thicket; and as Merrifield approached the dense tangle, the mortally wounded sow charged and he was forced to shoot the bear twice more before killing her. Merrifield then also killed the large cub.

Roosevelt was not nearly as foolish around grizzly bears as Merrifield. He'd read too many accounts of wounded grizzlies wreaking havoc on human flesh. However, he did note that a well-placed bullet would put down an unsuspecting bear in short order. A few years later Roosevelt encountered a grizzly that would change his mind. He had been hunting along the headwaters of the Salmon and Big Hole Rivers near the Idaho/Montana border with an old reprobate guide.

Theodore Roosevelt in a deerskin hunting suit

Finding the man drunk one evening, a disgusted Roosevelt set out on his own.

After setting up camp one evening along a small brook, Roosevelt set off to find a grouse or two for dinner. As the sun set, he decided to peek over the next hill before returning to camp. Easing to the crest of a low ridge, he spotted a large grizzly walking toward him. Roosevelt brought the rifle to his shoulder and fired, hitting the bear with a frontal quartering shot that pierced one lung. The bear let out a loud bawl and galloped back down the hill, with Roosevelt in close pursuit.

The bear entered a thicket, and Roosevelt gingerly circled it, hoping for a shot, but the bear burst out the far side.

What happened next is best told in Roosevelt's own words:

> The bear wheeled and stood broadside to me on the hillside, a little above. He turned his head stiffly toward me; scarlet strings of froth hung from his lips; his eyes burning like embers in the gloom. I held true, aiming behind the shoulder, and my bullet shattered the point or lower end of the heart, taking out a big nick. Instantly, the great beat turned with a harsh roar of fury and challenge, blowing the bloody foam from his mouth, so that I saw the gleam of his white fangs; and then he charged straight at me, crashing and bounding through the laurel bushes, so that it was hard to aim. I waited until he came to a fallen tree, raking him as he topped it with a ball, which entered his chest and went through the cavity of his body, but he neither swerved nor flinched, and at the moment I did not know that I had struck him. He came steadily on, and in another second was almost upon me. I fired for his forehead, but my bullet went low, entering his open mouth, smashing his lower jaw and going through the neck. I leaped to one side almost as I pulled the trigger; and through the hanging smoke the first thing I saw was his paw as he made a vicious side blow at me. The rush of his charge carried him past. As he struck he lurched forward, leaving a pool of bright blood where his muzzle hit the ground; but he recovered himself and made two more jumps onwards, while I hurriedly jammed a couple of cartridges into the magazine, my rifle holding four, all of which I had tried. Then he tried to pull up, but as he did so his muscles seemed suddenly to give way, his head dropped, and he rolled over and over like a shot rabbit.

That wasn't the last grizzly Roosevelt would kill, for he was an outdoorsman with a hunter's blood coursing through his veins, sending him on hunting expeditions to Africa and South America. But Teddy was, first and foremost, a naturalist. The excitement of the hunt came and went, but all aspects of the natural world keenly interested him, as did their travails.

For years he'd watched with growing frustration as greedy lumber barons made wastelands of ridges and mountainside of his home state of New York and neighboring Pennsylvania, leaving only stumps behind where great virgin stands of pine, hemlock, and oak had stood. And now, in North Dakota, he once again witnessed the exploitation of nature for monetary gain. Hide hunters had decimated a buffalo herd that once numbered 100 million, and by the time Roosevelt arrived in the West, buffalo were scarce. The once-thriving western elk herd had been reduced to a few pockets of animals that had managed to escape market hunters. And the grizzly, which Roosevelt called the lord of the wild kingdom, had ceased to exist in many of its former haunts.

In late 1887 he again took a hunting trip to his beloved Dakota Territory, where he found a still pristine landscape, but one devoid of wild animals. The antelope were all gone, as were the mule deer, the elk, even the grizzly. The tragedy dumbfounded Roosevelt, that the country could so quickly lose these noble animals he considered one of America's greatest legacies.

Upon his return to New York, he visited his friend George Grinnell, then editor of the prestigious *Forest & Stream* magazine. Together they founded the Boone & Crockett Club, dedicated to saving what was left of the country's big game animals and forests. With Teddy as its first president, the Boone & Crockett Club focused on Yellowstone National Park, created by Congress in 1872, where viable herds of elk, mule deer, antelope, and even the mighty grizzly bear could still be found. Unfortunately, there were no specific laws to protect the park from poachers and developers. Roosevelt became the motivational force behind the creation of the National Park Protective Act of 1894.

Finally, the national parks had laws, but during those early years there was almost no enforcement, nor any attempt to control developers. And Yellowstone was the worst. Because it still harbored the last vestiges of free-roaming wildlife, it became a target for meat and market hunters. The last remnant of America's buffalo herd was still hunted within park boundaries and slaughtered for hides! So also was the Rocky Mountain elk, already wiped out across most of its historic range on the Great Plains. The grizzly, extirpated across 90 percent of its historic habitat by the turn of the century, clung to a precarious existence in Yellowstone.

Roosevelt was no stranger to the world's first national park. His first of several visits came in 1886, and he immediately recognized its importance for a nation just awakening to the idea of conservation. As a result U.S. Cavalry M Troop arrived in Yellowstone under Captain Moses Harris and began meting out justice to market hunters and other exploiters, frontier style. Poachers were often thrashed and thrown in jail, where they sat for weeks, after which they were marched on foot scores of miles to the other side of the park and warned to not return, lest a worse fate befall them. With law and order finally in place, Yellowstone National Park blossomed into the natural wonderland it is today.

Calling Yellowstone a wilderness paradise, Roosevelt wrote:

> . . . every man who appreciates the majesty and beauty of the wilderness and of wild life, should strike hands with the farsighted men who wish to preserve our material resources, in the effort to keep our forests and our game-beasts, game-birds, and game-fish—indeed, all the living creatures of prairie and woodland and seashore—from wanton destruction.

During his time in the White House, Roosevelt established 150 national forests, the first fifty-five bird and game wildlife preserves, and five national parks. He also created the National Monument Act and set aside the first eight national monuments, including Devil's Tower, the Grand Canyon, and California's Muir Woods. In 1965, when the National Wildlife Federation established a Conservation Hall of Fame, Theodore Roosevelt was given its top honor, ahead of John James Audubon, John Muir, and Henry David Thoreau.

Though Roosevelt did not specifically target the grizzly for preservation, he most assuredly included the great bear in his wish list of endangered wildlife to be spared extinction. And while it is true that he hunted the great bear, he also called the grizzly the lord of the wilderness—the one wild animal who, much like himself, would give as much as it got when provoked.

Despite Roosevelt's tremendous conservation effort, it is a sad fact that men continued killing the grizzly in the years after his death in 1919, until the last scattering of great bears across the West were rooted out and shot, trapped, and poisoned. Only in Yellowstone and Glacier National Parks was the grizzly given legal protection that was actually enforced—at gunpoint if necessary. During those dark years for wildlife conservation from 1900 to 1960, Yellowstone and Glacier were the great bear's only sanctuary, and without them the grizzly may well have become extinct. Roosevelt made sure that didn't happen.

CHAPTER 3

⊶—⊷≡◈≣⊷—⊶—⊶≡◈≣⊶—⊶—⊶≡◈≣⊷—⊶

BUD CHEFF

LIVING AMONG INDIANS AND GRIZZLIES

On a late summer afternoon in 1924, a Salish Indian hunting party of two dozen men and women with children rode their horses up a steep mountain trail in western Montana's Swan Range, south of Glacier National Park. The group's leader, Philip Pierre, clad in traditional brown buckskin hunting shirt and leggings, urged his Appaloosa stallion up the rocky path. Deep wrinkles creased his burnished face, and graying hair pulled back in a tight braid attested to his age, but among the Salish there was no equal to his strength and prowess as a hunter.

When his friend Aeneas Conko had asked if they could bring a nine-year-old white boy along, Pierre had hesitated. The white government claimed these mountains, and the Indians were forbidden from seeking the old ways up here. Pierre smirked at such thinking. How could anyone own the mountains? Still, one word from the white boy, and the game wardens would come after them. They'd already killed several of his people for the crime of hunting on their own land.

The whites had brought his people nothing but misery and hardship, and the heat of anger flared within him for an instant; but he remembered that the boy, named Bud Cheff, had taken a keen interest in the old ways. He fashioned bows and arrows from creekside willows and hunted small game with the Indian boys. And he pestered the Salish elders about stories of the old days, especially about Sumka, *the great bear that roamed the high mountains above the Flathead Indian Reservation. A white Indian. . . . The thought intrigued Pierre and brought the hint of a wry smile to his cracked lips.*

Ahead, rugged granite peaks rose skyward to the heavens. Pierre thought of them as giant, brooding sentinels to protect his people. Now they cast long shadows, reminding him it was time to rest. Below the peaks, the forest leveled off and a lush alpine meadow with carpets of wildflowers beckoned. The grass up here, he knew, would still be sweet for the horses, and the nearby gurgling stream teemed with trout for supper. He closed his eyes and breathed in deeply, luxuriating in the soft scent of pine and the pungent aroma of huckleberries. Life, at least up here away from the madness of the reservation, was good.

Pierre felt the horse's muscles stiffen. He eased back the reins and the Appaloosa halted. The stallion, a veteran of many hunts, stared at a thicket of dark timber two rock throws to the left, its ears high and nostrils flared. It sniffed the air, and then softly snorted.

The others behind him waited in silence, except for the nicker of a young mare inexperienced in the hushed ways of the hunters. Pierre slid to the ground and affectionately rubbed the horse's ear, thanking his friend. He started forward, but paused under the mossy limbs of a great spruce tree. He turned back and stared at the white boy until their spirits met. With an urgent flick of his hand, he beckoned the boy to come forward.

Pierre led the way, slipping effortlessly through the shadows, but he kept a long, sinewy hand on the boy's skinny shoulder to make sure he did not stray. Pierre knew what lay ahead. He eased forward until amber-gold sunshine splashed upon his face at the edge of the meadow. He grasped the boy's arm to keep him from running, then brought him forward.

Young Bud Cheff's eyes bugged out. He gasped and cowered back. Just two rock throws away, three silver-tipped grizzly bears rooted and pawed at the meadow grass, their teeth snapping and lips smacking noisily as they devoured hordes of ladybug larvae among the wildflowers.

Cheff turned to the Indian leader and whispered urgently, "Will you shoot them?"

Pierre shook his head, but Cheff persisted. "Won't they kill us if they see us?"

A faint smile creased Pierre's leathery face. This would be the little white Indian's first lesson. He pointed a crooked finger at the feeding bears and said, "You no bother'um Sumka, Sumka no bother'um you."

Seventy-seven years later, I sat across the kitchen table from Bud Cheff in his rustic ranch house nestled among massive ponderosa pine trees at the base of the Mission Mountains. I felt thoroughly humbled and awed to be in the presence of a man whose life spanned an implausible stretch of time: from a time when the last free-roaming Indians clung to the old ways to our present high-tech cyber generation. I had grown to admire the historic Native-American ways by reading books. Now I sat in the presence of a man who'd walked the Indian path, who'd been taken in as one of their own, and whose tongue still tumbled out an occasional Salish word. As a testament to the bridge that Cheff had built between Indians and white men by using trust and respect, the Salish speak of him today with the reverence and respect afforded a tribal elder.

Though Cheff and I found a common ground in our admiration for the Native American culture, our passions also included the grizzly bear. Cheff had formed a kinship with the great bear by learning from the Indians how to live peacefully with this massive, lumbering beast they called Sumka. Through the years, Cheff's influence has spread to both Native-American and white society with a gospel of respect and understanding for the great bear and a spirit of restraint when man and beast cross paths.

The Cheff ranch is located in one of the most environmentally sensitive areas under private ownership along the western edge of the Rocky Mountains, a place where the grizzly struggles to maintain its presence in a land increasingly beset by civilization. This region become an oasis for resident grizzlies and the occasional bear that roams south from Glacier National Park, a safe place to rest and graze on grass among cattle and horses, or gorge on berries in creek bottoms before hibernation—all under the watchful eyes of Bud Cheff and his family.

Bud's parents, Viola and Marie Cheff, moved to the reservation in the early 1900s. Though officially French-Canadian, each had some Iroquois blood as well, but in those days were considered white. At that time, the Cheff family spoke only French, but soon learned enough Salish to communicate with their neighbors. In 1915 Bud was born, and the same year, an Indian child, Bill Conko, was born a short distance away. As soon as the boys could walk, they discovered each other and became inseparable. A narrow trail beaten bare by tiny moccasin prints ran from the Conko log cabin to the Cheff house.

Viola rented a piece of land from an old Indian named Teh Num Finley, a medicine man respected by all. Bud tagged along everywhere Teh Num went, and many Indians jokingly began calling Bud "Little Teh Num."

One night Teh Num's brother, Dave Finley, visited the Cheff house, and over dinner told a story of how he'd once been mauled by a grizzly bear. He was guiding a white man on a hunting trip near Mollman Pass in the nearby mountains when he saw a large grizzly bear walking on a ridge 60 yards above. The bear spotted them and began growling and popping its teeth, warning them to stay away. The hunter wanted to shoot the grizzly, but Finley whispered, "No! He's right above us. If you wound him, he'll be right on top of us!"

As Finley turned to leave, the hunter threw the gun to his shoulder and fired. The grizzly roared and bit at its shoulder, then galloped down the mountain straight for them. The hunter pushed Finley aside and ran yelling down the mountainside. Finley followed, but he'd only taken a few steps when a tremendous blow to his back sent him flying. The bear bit into his shoulder and shook him like a dog shakes a rat, tearing and ripping at his flailing arms and legs. With Finley on his back under the grizzly, the bear opened its mouth to bite his face, but the man shoved his fist into the bear's mouth, all the way up to the elbow, and grabbed the bear's tongue as he slipped into unconsciousness.

When Finley didn't arrive home that evening, friends and family mounted a search. They found him horribly mutilated and near death. While he lay in bed recuperating, Finley's rage burned hot for revenge against the man who had deserted him. As soon as he could get

Bud Cheff

around, he began searching for the coward, intending to kill him, but the man was smart enough to have fled the country.

Finley removed his buckskin shirt, exposing a right arm that was badly mangled, with deep, ripping scars running in all directions. The muscles on his back had been torn loose from the shoulder and now hung in fist-sized balls under the skin. Young Bud Cheff's eyes widened as he gaped at the horrible results of Finley's encounter with a grizzly, and a slow feeling of dread crept through his slim frame. If a grizzly could wreak such devastation on a grown man like Finley, what chance would he have against a bear? He would soon find out.

Bud encountered his first bear soon afterward. He and his brother were watering their horses at a creek a short distance from home when they looked back and saw a huge brownish bear standing in the trail watching them. Bud's horse spooked and ran off, with Bud running after it in terror. "At that time in my life, I couldn't tell a black bear from a grizzly," Bud remarked. "I just knew it was brown and had a rump as wide as a wagon. I still had the memory of Dave Finley's scarred body fresh in my mind, and I ran as fast as I could. Fortunately, the bear ran the other way."

Shortly after this encounter, Bud was invited by the Conko family to join the Indians on what would become his first of many hunting and gathering trips. That first night, Bud lay on a wool Indian blanket and stared at the stars—thinking about the three bears he'd seen and Pierre's words: "No bother'um Sumka, Sumka no bother'um you." And then he thought about Finley's scars, which seemed absolute proof that anyone who "bothered" Sumka ran the risk of getting themselves rearranged.

Bud reminisced as he stared out the kitchen window at the Mission Mountains, a wistful look on his weathered face:

> Those trips into the mountains were some of the happiest times of my life. The Indians were never sad. They were always laughing and smiling, even when they worked. The women picked roots and berries and nuts while the men scouted for large animals to hunt. On my first camping trip with them, the bucks shot several mountain goats. When they rode into camp with the meat, the squaws set up this big chorus of praise by clucking their tongues. You should have seen how proud those men were! The meat was cured over a low, smoky fire to preserve it for the pack trip home.

A faint smile plays upon Bud's lips as he continues, "Phillip Pierre threw this bloody chunk of meat at me. It was a piece of raw kidney.

Since all the other Indians accepted theirs with relish, I went along and popped mine into my mouth. I was surprised that even raw, it was tasty and chewy."

Though the Indians utilized all of what nature had to offer, they never ate grizzly bear meat. "I can't recall an Indian ever killing one," Bud mused. "Most of the Indians I knew felt a kinship toward the grizzly, and a lot of them thought the grizzly was the reincarnation of ancestors."

These early experiences with Native Americans set the tone for Bud's later attitudes of tolerance toward the many grizzly bears that lived in relative harmony with the early white settlers and Indians on the Flathead Indian Reservation. However, the calm was occasionally broken in an explosion of gunfire when one side or the other crossed the line. Such a transgression, and its bitter aftermath, occurred on the Cheff Ranch when Bud was thirteen years old.

Like most settlers in the West, the Cheff family subsisted on very little cash, with most of their sustenance coming from wild animals, home-grown vegetables, and a flock of sheep. One morning, Viola discovered that a bear had raided the sheep pen behind the house and killed four ewes.

Bud and his older brother, Rex, tracked the bear for several miles, hoping to put an end to the marauding bruin before it did more damage, but the big bear was a smart one. He knew he was being followed and stayed in the thickets. At sundown Bud and Rex hurried back to the ranch house and reassured their father they had chased the bear far enough away that the sheep would be safe. As a precaution, Viola penned the flock beside the house that night. Next morning, he stood in the sheep pen staring in bewilderment and rage at the carcasses of twenty-five sheep.

Viola then moved the flock a half mile away to the sheep shed, figuring that the bear wouldn't be able to get at them in the stoutly constructed log building. As a further precaution, Bud was stationed in the loft with his trusty single-shot 30-30 rifle.

Bud slept well that night—too well! When he climbed down from the loft next morning, he was stunned to find three dead sheep. The grizzly had climbed onto the roof sometime during the night and torn away enough cedar shingles to gain access. The bear had even carried a fourth sheep carcass out through the hole without disturbing Bud, who was sleeping soundly just 15 feet away!

Viola Cheff howled with anger when Bud quietly related the events of the night. He stalked into the barn and came back dragging an old no. 5 Newhouse bear trap. Bud and Viola followed the bear's trail and found where it had stashed the sheep carcass. Viola built a sturdy pen from logs and placed the sheep carcass at the back of the pen.

The bear trap, with its 16-inch jaw spread, was impossible to set by hand, so Viola used screw clamps to depress the powerful springs. He concealed the trap at the mouth of the pen, and then fastened the heavy trap chain to a green spruce log 10 inches thick and 8 feet long. The log would slow the bear down as it lunged to escape the trap, and would eventually become entangled in brush.

Early the next morning Viola rode out to check the trap and hurried back to the ranch with exciting news: The log pen had been demolished; the trap and drag were gone. Bud grabbed his rifle and hurried after his dad, who was carrying an old military 6mm rifle. Father and son followed the furrow of dirt left by the dragging log. They advanced only a short distance into a thicket of aspen trees when a furious bellow erupted and a huge silver-tipped grizzly reared up on its hind legs, the bear trap dangling off its right front paw. Viola snapped the rifle to his shoulder and shot the grizzly between the eyes. The massive bruin dropped like a sack of potatoes.

Viola gave the bear's massive head a few kicks, but when Bud started to take the trap off the bear's paw, Viola told him to wait because he was in a hurry to get back to the barn and bring out a horse and wagon. On their way back to the house, they met Bud's mom, Marie, and his two younger brothers. While Viola and Bud cleared a path to get the wagon into the thicket, Marie and the two children went ahead to see the dead bear.

A sudden roar ripped through the air, followed by more bellowing and the screams of Marie Cheff. While Viola searched frantically for his rifle (he'd left it back at the barn), Bud snatched up his little 30-30 and charged into the thicket, where he found his mother pulling the two children back as the big grizzly, now very much alive and pulling the drag along, bore down upon them. Bud stepped forward and, with the bear just 10 yards away and struggling furiously to get at him, placed the iron sights low on the animal's chest where the heart should be and squeezed the trigger. As the gunshot echoed through the mountains above, the big grizzly slumped to the ground at Bud's feet.

Marie and the children were hysterical, and Viola white as a sheet, especially when they discovered the grizzly was caught only by two toes! After the bear was skinned they discovered Viola's bullet had just gouged a furrow along the bear's forehead, knocking it out but not killing it.

Bud extended his gnarled hands to me during the interview and said, "After all these years, my palms still get sweaty every time I tell this story. I don't care how big and tough you think you are, when one of those big old grizzlies is in your face bellowing at you, it's enough to make anybody's hair stand on end."

Bud slowly shook his head and stared off into space for a few seconds before he spoke again. "I don't regret killing that bear. It had to be done. It was either us or him. But the next bear changed me forever."

Bud explained that in his later teens he took up with two other white kids who were into hunting and killing. One fall they rode their horses into a remote high country basin on the east side of the Mission Mountains to hunt elk. The boys split up, with Bud climbing to a secluded basin just below timberline. As he approached the meadow, he spotted a large silver-tipped bear moving through the trees on the other side of the opening. It was a huge brute, bigger than the bear his dad had trapped. For reasons that Bud to this day cannot explain, he raised the gun and fired.

The big grizzly leaped into the air and spun around and around, biting at his side and bellowing in pain before running off. Bud cautiously approached the area where the bear had disappeared, and found blood. He fetched his two hunting partners; they searched all day, but never found the bear. Bud's cohorts shrugged and reminded him that it was just a stinky old bear, so he shouldn't worry about it.

But Bud did worry about it. A lot. He finally confided in Aeneas Conko that he'd wounded a grizzly. Bud and Aeneas returned to the spot where he'd shot the bear. The Indian studied the area for a minute before pointing at a saddle a few hundred yards above. "Sumka go there."

They were still 100 yards from the saddle when the odor of putrid flesh hit them. Bud remembers the grim look on Aeneas Conko's face as he stared down at the rotting carcass. In a voice devoid of emotion, Aeneas grunted, "You want'um claws?"

Bud turned away, ashamed of himself. At that point in his life he was ready to throw his rifle away and never kill another living creature, but those were Depression years, and wild meat was necessary for a family to survive. Bud continued to hunt for subsistence, but he swore to Aeneas Conko that he would never kill another grizzly for "sport." It was not an idle oath. Bud Cheff never killed another grizzly for fun, striving instead to educate folks he encountered about the joy of seeing and communing with the great bear.

Bud's philosophy was sorely tested a few years later while he was guiding an elk hunter in the Holbrook drainage of the Bob Marshall Wilderness. Bud had led the hunter on horseback to a snow-covered meadow that held a mineral lick often frequented by elk. The men tied their horses in the trees about 200 yards from the meadow and sat on a log at the edge of the opening, waiting for a bull elk to appear.

A half hour later, Bud spotted movement in the timber near the horses. The hunter raised his rifle, ready to shoot, but when Bud identified the animal, he whispered, "Don't shoot. It's a grizzly!"

The big pale brown bear ambled along the trail they'd taken, nose to the ground like a dog. The men watched in amazement as the bear followed their circuitous route. Bud became increasingly nervous as the big bear moved closer and closer. Though the hunter did not have a bear license, he whispered excitedly, "I can kill him. I can kill him."

"No!" Bud adamantly shook his head. "I'll let him know we're here, and he'll run off."

The bear was just 30 yards away when Bud stood and waved his arms. "Go on now," he yelled. "Get out of here!"

The grizzly skidded to a halt and stood on its hind legs, cocking its massive head one way, then the other. The bear dropped down and advanced to within 15 yards before stopping again. "At this point, I was really spooked," Bud said. "This is the biggest bear I've ever seen, maybe 800 pounds. He's looking right at me, and I don't know whether it's a good look, or a bad look. I didn't have a gun, and I wasn't so sure the guy shaking in his boots beside me could even hit the bear if it charged."

Bud did not want to kill the grizzly, but neither did he want it to come any closer. Bud spoke in a low voice, "Go on now. Get on out of here. Nobody wants to hurt you."

Behind him, he heard the hunter stammer, "Do you want m-me to s-shoot?"

Bud slowly pushed down the rifle barrel and cautioned, "No, don't shoot."

For several minutes, bear and men stared at each other. Finally, the bear turned, lifted a hind leg and splashed a great volume of urine onto the ground. The grizzly slowly walked away, stopping several times to look back before it disappeared into the forest.

When the men got back to their horses, they found the animals unharmed, but nervous. The bear's tracks in the snow had come within 10 yards of the horses and circled them before taking up the human footprints. The hunter, rather than being disappointed, told Bud the bear encounter was the greatest thrill of his sporting life. Bud commented:

> I think that big old grizzly had never encountered humans before and was just curious. Lots of times people shoot a grizzly claiming self-defense when it comes toward them, but unless a bear shows some sign of aggression, I'm all for holding off shooting them.
>
> I've encountered hundreds of grizzlies in the mountains. Most of 'em'll move off as soon as they realize

you're there. Grizzlies just aren't interested in attacking humans. They seem to have an instinctive fear of us. You just have to let them know you're there and give them time to leave without feeling threatened. Surprising a bear is the worst thing you can do.

Bud raised a cautionary finger and added, "One other thing: Stay away from a sow with cubs. They're nothing to mess with. A sow will come right after you if she thinks her cubs are in danger."

Through the years the Cheff Ranch became a haven for bears. The encroachment of civilization, along with ranchers and hunters who were too quick to shoot every bear they saw, lowered grizzly numbers dramatically in the Mission Mountains. Bud explained:

> Me and my boys owned a big chunk of bottom land here along the western flank of the mountains, and we kinda set it up as a refuge for the bears to come down and feed on grass in the spring and eat berries along the creek in the fall. The bear research people came in here several times to do studies, that's how many bears we had.
>
> You might see a grizzly grazing in the pasture next to the house at any time. I've seen 'em everywhere around here. They really don't bother anything, and we leave them alone. All of us kinda like the idea of grizzlies roaming around the place. Just a couple weeks ago we had a dead cow at the far end of the pasture, and I was watching out the window when this big grizzly shows up and crawls under the barbed wire fence. He grabs that 800-pound cow and lifts the whole thing off the ground, then carries it over to the fence, drags it under the barbed wire and was gone. What a display of power! What a thrill to be able to see such a thing from your own living room window.

Bud's facial expression changed from euphoria to disgust as he continued:

> In the last couple years we've had to get secretive about the bears on our land just to protect them. Last year we

had a young sow grizzly den near the house. I even took the grandkids out in the winter and showed them the den. Next spring when that sow came out of the den, she headed for the green grass in a field where people could see her from the road. She only lasted a couple days before some idiot shot her from the road. Just killed her for the thrill of it and let her body lay there to rot.

Bud became pensive for a few seconds, gathering his thoughts.

I've spent many years camping and hiking in bear country. My opinion has always been that if you stay out of a bear's way, you'll be okay. I never worried about them, but I had a problem with a grizzly sow a while back that changed the way I act in grizzly country. It's made me more cautious. I don't just barge down trails anymore, especially if I know a bear's in the area.

Bud's moment of fate occurred one evening while he was guiding a hunter in the Bob Marshall's Burnt Creek area for elk. It had been a difficult week. A mule had kicked him in the right shoulder three days earlier, and he carried that arm in a sling. He'd also cut his good hand with a hatchet while splitting kindling.

The men followed fresh elk tracks up a ridge, but at sundown Bud suggested they give up the hunt; he did not relish field dressing an elk in the dark. As they hiked through a dense stand of lodgepole pine, Bud heard branches snapping below the ridge. He thought it might be the elk they'd been tracking, so he instructed the hunter to hurry down the ridge and find a good spot to wait, while he dropped below and tried to push the elk up to him.

Bud was about 200 yards from the ridge trail when he heard branches breaking below. He circled down lower, hoping to force the elk up to the hunter, but, when he stooped below some tree branches for a better look, he was startled to see four grizzlies galloping uphill toward him. Bud recalled:

The bears were real agitated. But I don't think they'd seen me yet. They were looking behind them, probably winded the other hunter, so I stood real still as they passed by 30 yards away. I thought everything was going to be okay, and then the sow cut my tracks. She spun around and around, huffing and snapping her teeth. Then she ran back towards me until she was about 60 yards away.

There I stood, with two bad arms, and a mad sow grizzly popping her teeth in front of me. I usually don't carry a gun when I'm guiding a hunter, but that day I had a little .22 revolver in case I saw a grouse. I knew I was in trouble if the sow saw me, so I started to climb a tree. The sow heard the noise and she went berserk, though she still didn't know where I was. Then I got the wild idea to let her know a human was in the area, so I yelled, "Hey, get the hell out of here!"

She went absolutely berserk, started bellowing and came right for me. There I was, only 6 feet up this skinny lodgepole pine tree with two bad arms, trying to load that little pistol.

I glanced over my shoulder and here she come barely 15 yards away. I dropped the pistol and tried to climb higher, but she leaped through the air and swatted me so hard on the upper thigh that I flew out of the tree.

I remember thinking while I was still flying through the air, "If this fall don't kill me, this sow's gonna finish the job as soon as I hit the ground." I landed on my back and got the wind knocked out of me. I just curled up and waited for the worst. After about a minute of cringing, it dawned on me that the bear wasn't tearing me apart. I slowly raised my head and saw the sow going out of sight with her cubs.

Besides his two bad arms, Bud now had a badly bruised butt and sore back as he limped back to his hunter, who stood trembling and wide-eyed. He'd heard the bear bellowing and Bud yelling and was sure that Bud was dead.

I tried to shrug the whole thing off, but that sow had spooked me like no other bear ever had. Back at camp the next night, I had to go out in the dark to feed the horses. Of course all I could think about was that big old sow. Well, we had this old dog that was so stove up she never left camp. Suddenly, I feel this animal nudge my sore butt, and I let out a big howl and the grain bucket went flying. It was just the dog.

Bud added empathically, "You can encounter lots of bears and spout off all you want, but after you've been swatted by a grizzly, it changes the way you act in the woods. I'm still not afraid of bears, but since that incident, I'm a lot more careful out there."

Our interview complete, Bud wants to get out in the fields. It's calving season. He grunts and winces as he struggles to stand, the result of ribs broken the week before when he tried to break up a horse fight. On the way out the door he puts on an ancient, sweat-stained cowboy hat.

"Grass is greenin' up," he says as he grabs a cracked leather halter off a fence post and gingerly starts for the horse corral. "I might see a grizzly this evening if these darn horses let me live long enough."

CHAPTER 4

BUD MOORE

YEARNING FOR THE GREAT BEAR'S RETURN TO THE BITTERROOTS

The Bitterroot Valley lies nestled against the eastern foothills of the mighty Bitterroot Range, a 200-mile string of steep timbered mountains and sheer rock peaks that form a seemingly impregnable divide between Idaho and Montana. When the Corps of Discovery passed through the valley, Captains Meriwether Lewis and William Clark wrote glowingly of the vast expanses of grassy meadows lying along the Bitterroot River and the amiable nature of the Salish Indians who lived there.

In the coming years white settlers moved into the valley and staked ownership to the most fertile lands. Conflicts arose between settlers and Native Americans, culminating in a forced march by the U.S. Army of the bewildered Salish Nation 100 miles north to the Flathead Indian Reservation.

With the Native Americans removed, farmers and ranchers quickly spread out through the Bitterroot Valley. But in the late 1800s much of the valley was also claimed by another native species—the grizzly bear. The pioneers quickly shot, poisoned, and trapped those bears that lived in the bottomlands and foothills, forcing the survivors to seek the solitude of the high country. Occasionally, a grizzly driven by hunger would slip down to the valley below, where just the sight of a bear grazing on meadow grass near stock or the discovery of a dead cow was enough to incite a new wave of extermination. Old-time trapper Johnny Richie caught nine grizzlies in two weeks for rancher Fay Humble in the upper Bitterroot Valley in 1870, and one of those bears weighed 950 pounds.

By the turn of the century, the remaining grizzlies on the eastern slopes of the Bitterroot Range in Montana survived deep within the rugged mountains. But in spring, when the bears emerged ravenous from hibernation, little food could be found in the snow-covered higher elevations where their dens were located, so they moved down to lower elevations to graze on spring grass or scrounge for winter-killed animals. Concentrated just below the receding snow line, the bears became easy prey for the trapper and his massive no. 5 and no. 6 Newhouse bear traps. Many of these trappers were old mountain men who'd hunted the buffalo to near extinction on the Great Plains and trapped the beaver out of most of the streams throughout the West.

A trapper caught a bear by first building a sturdy log pen. He then placed a 40-pound chunk of meat at the rear of the pen and set a bear trap at the entrance, concealing it with a covering of leaves and moss. All bears have a keen sense of smell, and the large bait, turning rancid in the warm spring sun, would exude even more odor and draw in any bear within a mile. The first bruin arriving at the log pen was almost certain to step into the trap.

But even the powerful jaws of a monstrous leghold trap often couldn't hold an enraged grizzly. Experienced trappers chained the trap to a stout drag pole about 10 inches in diameter and 8 feet long. The bear's first lunges would drag the pole along, allowing the steel jaws to sink deeper into the bear's flesh. As the trapped paw grew swollen, the bear descended into fatigue and shock. In time the dragging log would become entangled in brush or saplings, further securing the bear.

Wes Fales was one of the most successful bear trappers and hunters in the Bitterroot Mountains near the turn of the century. He spent the winter months trapping furbearers such as marten, lynx, and mink on the still wild, fur-rich Idaho side of the Bitterroot Mountains. Come March, Fales packed his furs over the divide and down Blodgett Canyon to the town of Hamilton, Montana, where he sold the furs and prepared for spring bear trapping.

The carnage wrought by men like Fales is best illustrated by one of

A typical log pen used for trapping bears

CENTER FOR WILDLIFE INFORMATION

his trap-checking trips during the spring of 1908. In the Hidden Fork of Big Sand Creek, on the Idaho side of the Bitterroots, Fales caught the big sow grizzly described at the beginning of chapter 1. After skinning out the sow, he left the remaining two cubs wailing beside their mother's carcass and packed the bear's hide and the third squealing cub to his cabin on Blodgett Creek, where he spent a peaceful night asleep with the cub stuffed into a small coal-oil box.

The next morning Fales started down Blodgett Creek toward Hamilton, checking bear traps as he went. One trap held a large black bear, which he killed and skinned. Another trap held a big grizzly that had dragged the trap away. While following the drag trail, Fales spotted a feeding grizzly. He shot and wounded the bear, which escaped. Returning to the business of tracking the trapped bear, he followed the marks of the drag log for three days before he finally stumbled upon the bear in deep snow. Near-

75

*mad with pain, the animal turned on its tormentor and charged, but Fales
shot it. During all this time the grizzly cub remained crammed inside the
coal-oil box. Fales finally hiked out to Hamilton with the cub and returned
the next day with a horse to retrieve the three bear hides.*

Compared to today's environmentally enlightened standards, these
anecdotes read as wanton examples of senseless slaughter of the grizzly, but at the beginning of the twentieth century, such exploits were
apt to be applauded by farmers and ranchers in the Bitterroot Valley.
With men like Wes Fales and upwards of ten other bear trappers working the Bitterroots, more than forty grizzlies were killed annually.

By the time a man named Bill Moore settled his family on a rustic
eighty-acre homestead a dozen miles up Lolo Creek—the drainage that
Lewis and Clark had traversed on their journey to the Pacific Ocean—
most of the grizzlies on the Montana side of the Bitterroot Mountains
had been killed off.

Times were tough during those early years on the Moore homestead, with little work for Bill to provide for his family. So Bill came up
with a rather unconventional occupation: He began to make moonshine. Prohibition was in force during the 1920s, creating a flourishing
industry of illegal whiskey makers, who plied their trade in well-hidden
hollows where they distilled grain into raw alcohol, often called moonshine. Bill found a ready market for his product a dozen miles to the
north in the bawdy frontier town of Missoula. It was into this humble,
yet vibrant and sometimes chaotic, world that Bud Moore was born in
1917.

On a warm afternoon in May 2004, I arrived at Bud Moore's cozy
log cabin nestled deep in the forest 5 miles back from the highway in
western Montana's Swan Mountains. After pouring me the first of what
would be a dozen cups of coffee, Bud began to explain how he grew
from a backwoods waif into one of the most visible and strident proponents of the grizzly in the Bitterroots.

I couldn't have asked for a better childhood. From my
earliest memories, I was out in the woods fishing and

hiking. By the time I was six years old I was following along behind my Dad and his mountain man friends on hunting and fishing trips. Back then, we lived at the edge of the wilderness. Many's the time my dad would jump out of bed at night when some varmint came sneaking into the barnyard, causing the livestock to go crazy. Dad would just blast away into the night with his rifle, and I wouldn't doubt that some of those midnight marauders back in the early 1920s were some of the last grizzlies in Lolo Creek.

Bill Moore also found a steady clientele for his moonshine among the mountain men who stopped by for a meal and bed. Bud reminisced:

Those were real mountain men. They were leftovers from the old days. Some of them were old buffalo hunters, some trappers. All of them were coming or going to the Idaho side of the Bitterroot Range, where it was still wild and free. After my Mom fed them, they'd sit around the table and Dad would bring out a jug of his moonshine and pour each one a cup. I just loved sitting off to the side and listening to those old mountain men tell their stories.

Most of them were coming out of the Lochsa, the main river drainage on the Idaho side of Lolo Pass. The Montana side was getting pretty well settled, so those old-timers spent most of their time hunting and trapping in Idaho where it was still wilderness. I'd sit quietly and listen for hours to them talk, and the more moonshine they drank the louder they got. They talked about a land still in its natural state, full of deer and elk. But eventually their talk turned to the big bears over on the Idaho side—grizzlies 1,000 pounds or more. Every mountain man had a half dozen grizzly stories and I'd soak in every one of them. Those men seemed, not in awe, but respectful of the grizzly.

Bud mentioned that he made friends with an old buffalo hunter named Joe Draper, who lived up Lolo Creek.

I'd visit old Joe and listen to his stories of hunting vast herds of thousands of buffaloes and living among free-roaming Indians. Joe just loved to talk about those old days. He gave me my first rifle, a .22 Stevens rolling block. Years later he also gave me a 45-70 dropping block Springfield. Joe still had his big Sharps buffalo gun. I really wanted that gun, but it disappeared as Joe got older.

Unfortunately, Bill Moore's lucrative moonshine trade ended at dawn one morning when government agents descended upon the Moore homestead, found the still, and made an example of Bill Moore with a one-year jail sentence. Overnight, eight-year-old Bud Moore became the provider for his family. He told me:

I'd bring along my old 30-30 Winchester with me to school. I'd hide it in a hollow stump and then hunt my way home. One day I spotted a big black bear along the banks of Lolo Creek. I shot the bear, my first, and my mother was so excited to get all that meat and lard, and we sold the hide.

With the return of Bud's dad from prison came the return of the mountain men to the Moore homestead. "I believe those mountain men especially admired the charisma of the grizzly," Bud mentioned, then added:

But they were also hunters of the bear. They harvested surplus bears to sell their hides, and they ate the meat. And, of course, they never had any idea that their actions could some day bring about the demise of the grizzly. At that time, there was just too much wilderness in Idaho; too many grizzlies over there.

Those mountain men were almost totally uneducated, but they were the first true conservationists and ecologists because they saw the entire wilderness as one big functioning ecosystem, with themselves being a part of it. They knew there were connections and interconnec-

Bud Moore exploring grizzly habitat near the
crest of the Bitterroot Range

PHOTO COURTESY BUD MOORE

tions to nature, but they didn't have the depth of scientific knowledge to understand how it all tied together. They just trimmed surplus animals and made sure that there was seed for next year.

The mountain men left an indelible mark on young Bud Moore. While other boys at the country schoolhouse dreamed of riding in a gleaming Ford Model T or flying in a biplane, Bud's daydreams were of that faraway land that the mountain men called God's Country and the thrill of one day encountering the mighty grizzly bear that ruled the wild Lochsa country.

79

Though the grizzly had been killed off in the lower elevations of Lolo Creek, a few bears still wandered over the divide from Idaho. One time Bud became an unwitting participant in a grizzly bear hunt.

> I was out hunting deer with two other kids from school. We were on opposite sides of a draw when one of the kids spotted a grizzly right in front of me. He raised his gun and started shooting at the bear. It looked like he was pointing at me, so I hid behind a tree while he was shooting.

Fortunately, the excited lad's aim was off and the grizzly escaped.

> My dad got real upset when he heard about the other kid shooting at the grizzly right in front of me. He knew what danger I could have been in if the bear had been wounded so close to me. Dad had always pretty much let me run free, but he put some stringent restrictions on my hunting trips that fall. One other boy could accompany me, but I had to be the leader. If more than one boy wanted to go, I had to stay at home.

Bill Moore had reason to be cautious when it came to the grizzly, for he knew that the bear, though normally reclusive and anxious to retreat when given the chance, could also turn into a fearsome adversary when provoked or wounded. Undoubtedly Bill remembered what had happened to a trapper named Lawrence, the first white settler who lived in Lolo Creek with his Nez Perce Indian wife. The Indians called him Lawrence Lou Lou, later modified to Lolo, thus the origin of this famous name. In 1853 Lawrence and an Indian companion encountered a grizzly bear on a trail near his home, located not far from the Moore homestead. Lawrence shot, but only wounded the bear. The Indian quickly climbed a tree to escape the enraged animal; but Lawrence was too old to climb, and the grizzly attacked him. The Indian shot enough arrows at the grizzly to drive it off the severely wounded Lawrence, but he died a short time later.

Bud Moore explained:

Us kids had a lot of freedom and independence in those days. When I was twelve years old I'd already covered every draw, every mountain, and every trail in the Lolo Creek drainage. I'd heard so much about the big wilderness on the Idaho side of the border. I wanted to go there and experience what the mountain men called God's Country. The summer I was twelve years old I asked my dad if I could go over there and explore the Lochsa and he said yes. It took me two days to get to the border, but what a sight it was to see that wild Idaho country stretching out as far as the eye could see. It drew me like a magnet, down the steep mountainside and into the Brushy Fork of the Lochsa River.

The Lochsa was such remote country in those days. The deeper I went into the wilderness, the greater this intense feeling of loneliness became, but it was not a scary thing. More exciting than anything, like I was Lewis and Clark discovering the land. Of course, I knew better. I was following an old trapline trail with blaze marks on the trees leading from marten set to set, which consisted of a notch chopped out of the side of a tree where the trapper had placed a small baited trap for a marten.

It was getting on towards dusk when I came across a huge bear track at a bog hole. The track was fresh. There was muddy water in the pug marks. The bear was somewhere just ahead. My old Winchester never felt so good in my hands, but I also felt a little intimidated because it was such a small gun for protection from such a big bear. With all the wild bear stories of those old mountain men running through my mind, I eased forward, examining the long claw marks left by the bear in the mud as I went. When I climbed onto a low, rocky ridge, I figured the bear might have wandered off the trail, but then a movement ahead startled me. It was a big grizzly. It came toward me and stopped about 30 feet away, stood on its hind legs and sniffed the air. I can still see that short nose loudly sniffing at the air. And then it was gone. Just like that it had disappeared.

Bud's expression became florid and a wry smile spread across his face as he remembered.

Oh, I was scared! My knees were knocking and my hands shook. I doubt I could have shot that bear if it came back, but I was excited too. Here I was, a twelve-year-old kid and this big grizzly had run away from me. It was a defining moment in my life because I realized right then and there that I wanted to spend my time in this vast wilderness, and I wanted the grizzly to be a part of it.

Bud was right about the wildness of the place. The Lochsa country in 1930 was a true wilderness, one of the few remaining in the lower forty-eight states. Other areas in the West had larger expanses of uninhabited land, and maybe even more pristine and picturesque landscapes, but they lacked the ecological balance that only the Lochsa and a handful of other areas possessed: a true balance of nature, with the grizzly at the top of the food chain. While remnant populations of grizzlies were being exterminated in the Southwest and Northwest, including nearby areas of Montana and Idaho, the Lochsa, because of its wonderful supply of protein-rich salmon, allowed the grizzly to flourish and maintain its population density at a time when most other areas of the West were bereft of the great bear.

Unfortunately, the world beyond the wild Lochsa country was rapidly changing—and for the grizzly, not for the better. A hydroelectric dam was constructed at Lewiston, Idaho, on the Clearwater River, the main tributary of the Lochsa. Fish ladders were installed on the dam, but initially they did not operate effectively and eliminated most of the spring and summer spawning runs of salmon up the Clearwater and Lochsa Rivers. Grizzlies for many hundreds of years had relied upon this seasonally abundant food supply; now they emerged from hibernation and wandered in bewilderment along the banks of the Lochsa, Clearwater and Selway Rivers, which held not a single salmon.

At about the same time, the Western Montana Livestock Association began sending thousands of sheep up through the Bitterroots into Idaho's Elk Meadows country and other grasslands along the state line that were created when a devastating wildfire in 1910 burned off much of the dense old-growth forest, allowing grass to flourish. Local ranchers also took advantage of these new grasslands and sent their cattle to the high country to grow fat in summer.

The silence of the wilderness was now interrupted by the maddening bleats of thousands of sheep and the bellowing of cattle. And in this land roamed the hungry grizzly. The sudden disappearance of the salmon coupled with the appearance of dim-witted sheep and cattle proved irresistible to the predators. Though no one—including young Bud Moore—knew it at the time, these events would prove disastrous for the great bear. In fact, Bud would unwittingly play a part in one tragic episode.

Bud was thirteen years old when the first great herd of more than 1,000 sheep came bleating into the Bitterroots in the summer of 1931. He was hired as a herd tender for $15 per month by a sheep man who was taking his flock over the Bitterroot Divide into Idaho's Elk Meadows. Thus Bud took part in the first dramatic invasion of domestic stock into the Lochsa country.

In August the other herder and cook quit, leaving Bud to tend the sheep alone in the mountains. Bill Moore hiked into Elk Meadows to spend a few days with his son. One day, while they were moving the sheep to new pasture, nightfall overtook the flock in dense, blown-down lodgepole pine. The sheep bedded down there, and the two men could not camp as close to them as usual. That night a big bear ravaged the flock, killing thirty sheep and eating only the hearts and livers of a few.

As Bill surveyed the carnage, he spoke somberly to Bud. "You know we're going to have to kill this bear, don't you?"

Bud sadly nodded.

"If we don't," the elder Moore added, "It'll just keep coming back."

It took most of the day to gather the terrified sheep together again. While Bud and the sheep dogs guarded the flock that evening, Bill saddled his horse and galloped off into the night for home. The next day he returned with a no. 6 Newhouse bear trap.

Father and son constructed a rough pen using young trees and placed several sheep carcasses inside. Bill carefully set the big trap and concealed it at the entrance, taking care to cover the steel jaws and the heavy chain under bear grass. They checked the trap the next day. Nothing. Neither was the pen disturbed the next day, nor the next. For five days there was no activity. The sheep had devoured most of the surrounding pasture, and it was time to move them. They'd remain another day, then pull the trap and move the flock.

After the sheep had bedded down at midday, Bud and Bill hiked to the set. They were stunned to find a half-acre area of forest destroyed. Sheep carcasses were strewn in all directions and the lodgepole thicket had been flattened, with trees pulled out of the ground by their roots.

As Bud gasped at the carnage, his dad muttered, "We got him."

They followed the drag marks left by the heavy log chained to the trap, but lost the trail near a meadow. Bill unleashed the three sheep dogs and the animals shot off through the forest, with the two men trying their best to keep up. A minute later a series of terrific bellows ripped through the air.

Bill kept Bud behind him as they eased forward. There, between two large spruce trees, stood a huge, silver-tipped grizzly bear. With the trap fastened to its right front paw, the bruin stood on its hind legs and held trap, chain, and log drag off the ground while it took vicious swings at the dogs with its other paw. Each time the dogs backed off, the bear would drop down, bellowing and snapping its jaws. When the dogs moved in, the huge brute would stand up to face them.

Bill's voice rose above the cacophony of yapping dogs, snapping jaws, and bear bellows. "Do you want to shoot him?"

Bud's hands were shaking so much he could barely grasp the rifle. He studied the bear for a few seconds before replying, "No, you go ahead." Father and son's eyes met. Bill knew how much his son admired the great bears, and his reply was a nod of understanding. He snapped his rifle to his shoulder, and the big bear collapsed at the roar of the rifle. Only then did Bud step forward to put a bullet behind the bear's ear to make sure it was dead.

"Whew!" Bill emitted a low whistle as the men stood over the battle-scarred boar, a huge dark brown brute with silvery frosting of guard hairs running along his back. "He must weigh at least 1,000 pounds."

That was the only bear killing that Bud Moore ever had a hand in, but others had no such qualms. After the 1932 grazing season, Bud found nine bear scalps nailed to a tree near Packer Meadows. Through the 1930s sheep men killed many bears. And not just sheep killers. Any bear became a dead bear if it stood still long enough to allow a man to draw a rifle bead on it. Likewise, cattlemen killed any bear seen near their stock.

With the salmon gone, the remaining grizzlies began to roam far beyond their traditional range in the Lochsa in search of food. Trouble, and often death, followed them. One big grizzly wandered over the divide into Montana and raided rancher Ted Williams's sheep pen one night. Williams shot the bear as it was leaving the pen with a ewe in its jaws.

The fledgling U.S. Forest Service had been making inroads into the Lochsa country during those years and had built several small log cabins at strategic points. Well stocked with food, they often became a favorite target for marauding bears. Retribution quickly followed. Many grizzlies were trapped or shot after being brought to bay by hunting hounds.

During the 1930s Bud worked seasonally for the U.S. Forest Service in the Lochsa country, then trapped furbearers in the winter. He saw with his own eyes the rapid demise of the grizzly. Bears were being killed everywhere—for preying on livestock, for breaking into cabins, and sometimes just for being a grizzly. In his reminiscence Bud mentions that in just ten years the grizzly was largely wiped out of the Lochsa. In those early years of his forest service career, he had little authority to stop, or even slow, the numerous grizzly killings. Bud rose quickly through the forest service hierarchy, and in 1949 was promoted to ranger at the Powell Ranger District, giving him authority over U.S. Forest Service management decisions in that area.

But even that status did not furnish Bud with enough power to halt the great bear's decline. He would hear word of a bear being shot here and another grizzly shot there. He scoured the Lochsa country for grizzly sign. The last grizzly track he located was in the Spruce Creek Fork of the Brushy Fork of the Lochsa in 1946.

Grimly determined to fight the extinction of the grizzly in the Lochsa, Bud refused to admit defeat. Through the 1940s, Bud's annual reports continued to show a population of five grizzlies in his district. But eventually his sense of professionalism and the increasing skepticism of his superiors forced him to face his worst fears: The grizzly was gone. "Some land manager," he quipped as we sipped coffee.

I was the ranger at the Powell Ranger District when the grizzly officially became extinct in the Lochsa.

That was back in the 1950s, and in those days the idea of bringing back the grizzly was as foreign as putting a man on the moon. The philosophy among Forest Service land managers concerning the grizzly was: "When they're gone, they're gone."

Something died in me when I made my annual wildlife report and added a zero next to the grizzly bear. I really wasn't interested in being in a place where the grizzly was absent. It wasn't the same. It didn't have the same feel. The grizzly was gone. What a tragedy. Not only that, but the Lochsa was being roaded up with logging and recreation roads. Then we had this big spruce budworm epidemic. The worms were harming young spruce trees, so the Forest Service sprayed those areas with DDT. We killed the budworms alright, but we killed all the other insects, too, and the birds that fed on them, and the frogs and the fish in the waters where the DDT ended up. [Six years later, Rachel Carson would write her epic book, *Silent Spring*, which sounded the alarm about the effects on the food chain of pesticides and other chemicals.] For me, it was time to leave. It just wasn't the same anymore.

Bud left the Lochsa in 1957, transferring from the wild rainforests of the Lochsa country to the concrete jungles of Washington, D.C, where he pioneered fire-management practices that are still in use today. Bud's body was far from the Lochsa, but his heart was always back there. In his stuffy bureaucratic confines, Bud's mind often wandered back to his boyhood homestead in Lolo Creek, with the mountain men who bragged about their traplines and the big grizzlies they'd encountered, and the absolute beauty and awe of a land so special that he physically ached over its demise.

Bud retired from the forest service to write the Lochsa story, and he spent several years traveling across the country interviewing people for the book. One of his most interesting interviews involved a woman named Margaret Gorsky, then the ranger at Powell Ranger Station.

"I visited Margaret at her home in the summer of 1990. While we were sipping coffee at her kitchen table she come right out and asks me, 'Why did you kill the last grizzly in the Lochsa?' I almost fell out of my chair!"

"Well, the records say you did," Margaret replied. "An entry in 1950 states that you killed a big grizzly in Cold Creek in 1950. That's the last grizzly death we have on record."

Bud searched his memory for a few minutes before replying.

Okay, I remember now. Here's what happened. A man stopped by the Ranger Station and told me that someone had killed a big bull moose in Cold Creek and left it. I hiked in there to retrieve the antlers. When I got to the place where the moose was supposed to be, I stepped over a spruce log and came face-to-face with a big black bear guarding the carcass just 10 yards away. The bear bristled and started snapping its jaws at me. I shot it from the hip, and it pitched over backwards. I packed both the moose and the big black bear out and filled out a report on the incident. Somehow, the "Big Bear" became a grizzly.

In 1996 Bud's book *The Lochsa Story* was published by Mountain Press of Missoula, Montana, and became a bestseller. The book is required reading for anyone, from private citizen to professional land manager, who is interested in learning how man has the capability to protect and improve the environment, or misuse and damage it.

And then, beginning in 1998, Bud began hearing rumors about the possibility of reintroducing grizzlies to the Bitterroot ecosystem. At first he dismissed such reports as nothing more than rumors. After all, the old forest service adage had been: "When they're gone, they're gone."

But if they could put a man on the moon, why couldn't they put grizzlies back in the Bitterroots? Bud learned that the U.S. Fish & Wildlife Service, as mandated by the Endangered Species Act, was indeed studying the Bitterroot ecosystem as one of seven areas suitable for the reintroduction of the grizzly. "I can't even describe the emotions that swept over me when I found out it was true," Bud told me. He remained silent for several seconds, staring intensely into my eyes, before he added in a soft voice, "It was just like a part of me that had died had been reborn."

The Bitterroot Grizzly Bear Reintroduction Plan called for five nonproblem surplus bears from Canada and the United States to be reintroduced to the Selway-Bitterroot Wilderness Area beginning in the summer of 2002, and continuing with five seed bears being released each year for the next five years, with a target recovery population of about 200 bears over the next century. Wildlife professionals worldwide hailed the plan as critically needed to link the Yellowstone grizzly population to the east with the grizzly enclaves in Glacier National Park and the nearby Swan and Cabinet Mountains.

Anxious to make this plan a truly grassroots movement, the U.S. Fish & Wildlife Service took the extraordinary step of recommending the formation of a citizen's committee comprising twelve Montana and Idaho residents, to oversee the Bitterroot Grizzly plan.

By the year 2000 the grizzly reintroduction plan had run the administrative gauntlet and was overwhelmingly approved by 97 percent of America. When I spoke with Bud in the spring of that year, he was ecstatic about the imminent return of the grizzly. "I just got a phone call from Chris Servheen [Bitterroot grizzly reintroduction coordinator]. In my honor he said he'd like me to accompany him and release the first grizzly back into the Bitterroots. Oh, what a grand day that will be!"

But the year 2000 was also an election year. New Republican President George Bush quickly went about repaying political debts, one of which was to the Republican governor of Idaho. In the spring of 2001, newly appointed Secretary of Interior Gale Norton announced that the administration would table the grizzly bear reintroduction program for the foreseeable future while the issue was "re-evaluated." The term "re-evaluated" in political-speak means "killed." And with no set date for the re-evaluation process to be completed, this is exactly what happened.

Bud shook his head while speaking of the political intrigue surrounding the grizzly reintroduction effort.

> I attended several meetings that were hostile and full of fear-mongering toward the grizzly, but the people respected me when I spoke of my experiences with the wild grizzly. I think it registered when I told them that in all the years I'd traveled the Bitterroots, I saw only five grizzlies. There was that first bear in Idaho. Then I walked into a grizzly on a trail in the South Fork of Lolo Creek on the Montana side. That bear stood on its hind legs, popped its jaws a couple times and ran off. Then in Idaho I saw bears three other times when I hiked into Elk Meadows and Skookum Lake.

Today, the vast 16.1-million-acre Bitterroot ecosystem harbors stately ponderosa pines towering 200 feet above the forest floor. There are alpine meadows and breathtakingly beautiful snow-capped peaks. Royal bull elk grace the high country, and bighorn sheep and mountain goats cling to rugged peaks above. There are whitetail and mule deer, coyotes, and now even wolves. There are lots of black bears.

But no grizzlies.

At the time of this writing, Bud Moore is pushing ninety years of age, but he continues, through his writing and public appearances, to extol the virtues of the wilderness land ethic and the return of the great bear. We can only hope that, before he joins Trapper Lawrence and his dad and those mountain men who stopped by the homestead almost a century ago, he might have the honor of opening the cage that sends the first grizzly bear bounding away through the bear grass at Elk Meadows.

CHAPTER 5

HOWARD COPENHAVER

LOVING WILDERNESS AND GRIZZLIES

Howard Copenhaver's matchstick-thin legs churned over the forest floor, spurred on by the heavy thud of massive paws pounding the ground behind him. He shot a glance back and saw only the gaping maw of the enraged grizzly.

A limbless lodgepole pine loomed ahead. Without slowing down, Howard leaped up, wrapped his arms and legs around the trunk, and frantically shinnied up it. But neither did the grizzly slow down at the tree. Carried forward by its enormous bulk, the great bear lunged upward for the man.

At the last second Copenhaver pulled up his legs, and the bear's jaws snapped shut inches short of his right boot. Then gravity took over and the bellowing bear flailed at the air as it fell backward, hitting the ground with a heavy thud and a loud grunt. The bear was back on its feet in a flash, biting at the tree and glowering up at Howard before finally stalking back to its food cache. The grizzly lay on the carcass of the dead bull elk, baleful eyes studying Copenhaver between bites.

Though Copenhaver allowed himself a sigh of relief, he knew his ordeal was far from over. The bear was just 30 yards away, and the man figured he would have to make a similar mad dash for a new tree, and later another, before he was far enough away that the bear would leave him alone.

I sat in Howard's living room in Ovando, Montana, in April 2003, mesmerized not only by his tale but also by the array of animals and birds surrounding us. These were not so much trophy adornments as a shrine to wilderness. On the wall beside me sat a pine marten mounted on a branch. A mallard duck took wing on the opposite wall. A wolverine rug adorned the wall behind Howard, with a badger skin beside it. A mule deer head and a standing whitetail were to his left, and above him hung a mature golden eagle, its spread wings slowly turning in the blue haze of cigarette smoke. My attention, however, was riveted to the huge grizzly bear rug draped over the couch where Howard sat. After listening with bated breath to Howard's story—his mad scramble, the bear's murderous rush, the jaws snapping just inches short—I pointed at the bear hide and asked, "Is that the bear, Howard?"

"You mean Slewfoot?" Howard grinned and patted the bear rug. "Naw, it wasn't Slewfoot. Me and Slewfoot's old friends. We've known each other for more than twenty years."

Howard jumped to his feet and disappeared into a back bedroom. A minute later he returned with a huge bear skull and handed it to me. "See here," Howard said and pointed at a hole in the jawbone where the lower right canine should have been.

> That's how I first met Slewfoot back in 1946 in the North
> Fork of the Blackfoot River. I returned to my hunting camp
> one evening and the place was all tore up. A big sow and
> two cubs, one of them limping, ran off. When I picked up
> one of the cast-iron lids to the woodstove, the hole where
> you stick the poker in to pick it up had a small bear's
> tooth and a piece of the jawbone stuck in it. I guessed the
> cub bit at the lid and got its tooth stuck in the hole. That's
> how I knew Slewfoot's work, by his bite marks and his
> turned-in paw print. In the twenty-six years I knew ol'
> Slewfoot, I'd guess he raided my hunting camps maybe
> forty times. But that's another story. Back to the bear that
> chased me up the tree.

"You must have been terrified during your ordeal with that bear," I commented.

Howard lit another cigarette and blew a plume of blue smoke upward, sending the eagle slowly spinning. "Naw, I wasn't scared. After what I've seen men do to other men during the war, there wasn't nothing a big ol' grizzly could do to scare me."

Howard was referring to the events surrounding the morning of December 7, 1942, a day then-President Roosevelt proclaimed "would live in infamy." As the sun rose above the horizon on that beautiful day, Howard stood on the USS *Maryland*'s deck gazing down at the warm, blue-green waters of Pearl Harbor. He was a twenty-eight-year-old backcountry boy from Montana who had taken leave from his outfitting business in the heart of the game-rich Bob Marshall Wilderness Area in western Montana, a land so beautiful and sacred to his soul that Howard claimed only his love of country could have pried him away.

"When the planes appeared as tiny dots on the horizon," Howard explained, "no one thought anything of it because there was planes flying around all the time. Then the noise got louder and louder, and the alarm sounded and I headed below deck at the call to man battle stations."

The first wave of Japanese bombers dropped torpedoes that tore through the Pacific Fleet's aircraft carriers. And then the dive bombers appeared high in the sky. Two 500-pound bombs hit the *Maryland,* and that's all Howard remembered until he regained consciousness while being pried away from the tangled steel and pulpy flesh that had minutes ago been his fellow seamen.

"The doctors said I wouldn't walk again, and even if I did, I'd be in a wheelchair by the time I was forty years old." Howard sucks in a deep drag from his cigarette and says with a sly grin, "That was fifty years ago."

After months convalescing in a military hospital, Howard Copenhaver returned to his beloved Bob Marshall country. Not only could he walk, but when a big grizzly was snapping at his heels, he might have set a world record in the forest sprint.

But mostly, he rode a horse. The Blackfoot River country, made famous by Norman Maclean's *A River Runs Through It,* was a wild, raw land inhabited by tough men with an aversion to wimps. So it is doubly amazing that Howard Copenhaver would not only fit in but would also come to personify the toughness of the men who plied their trade guiding "dudes" on elk and bear hunting trips.

Howard certainly was no "Marlboro Man." At 5 feet 8 inches tall, he was rail-thin at 135 pounds and spoke in a soft voice that often raised an octave to be heard. But what the man lacked in physical stature, he made up for with sheer toughness, hard work, outdoor savvy, and horse logic. Rodeo was the main form of entertainment in the sparsely settled regions of the West, and Howard became a champion bareback bronc rider. Of course the other cowboys complained good-naturedly that Howard was cheating because there wasn't enough of him to get the horse upset.

Eventually, the open range throughout western Montana began to disappear, as barbed wire choked off the lifestyle of the free-roaming cowboy. Like many a cowboy looking for extra work, Howard took to outfitting. His horse savvy, along with his disarming appearance and easygoing manner, made him one of the most respected men who roamed the vast Bob Marshall Wilderness that stretched south from Glacier National Park for almost 50 miles. Well-connected men from the upper echelons in the East Coast and European society often chose to hunt with Howard, whose easygoing manner and impromptu storytelling talents made him a favorite of the affluent.

Howard differed from the other outfitters and cowboys on one subject—grizzly bears. Just the subject of grizzlies was enough to make the average cowboy kick the dirt and spit a chaw of tobacco onto the ground before sharing a tale of a grizzly seen, and a grizzly shot. "It wasn't just the cowboys back then," Howard explained.

> Just about everybody was killing them. In those days there wasn't many grizzlies around. There'd be maybe one or two seen all year, probably surplus bears coming south

Howard Copenhaver

from Glacier. And more often than not it was, "Look, there's a grizzly, BANG!" I just didn't see it that way. We were living in the greatest corner of the world. The Bob [slang for the Bob Marshall Wilderness] was a sportsman's paradise, filled with bighorn sheep, mountain goats, whitetail and mule deer, thousands of elk, and hundreds of black bears. The way I saw it, the one animal missing from a perfect world up there was the grizzly. But old habits die hard. The people back then was raised to shoot every bear they saw. Many's the time I stood around a campfire in the Bob listening to the other cowboys bemoan the loss of the free days of the open range, and I'd say, "Then why are you trying to do the same thing back here in the Bob by killing off the grizzly? He's just like us, the last of the truly wild and free wild animals."

The older guys who grew up hating bears scoffed at me and kept on killing every bear they saw, but some of the younger guys listened. I mentored lots of young men looking to find a niche in some of the last free life in the country, and I'd say to them, "How can you sell the Bob to some eastern sportsman as the last true intact wilderness when you go and kill off the greatest animal out here?" I'd tell them, "Next time you see a grizzly, instead of shooting it, just sit back and watch it for a while and think of what some bank president would say if he was sitting at your side, and you were showing him the last wild animal in the world that isn't afraid of man."

As the old-timers got too old to work as outfitters and the younger guys took their places, fewer bears were shot. The grizzly was really making a comeback. Then disaster struck. Howard explained:

It was back in the 1950s, and the forest service got this wild idea about leasing some of their property to sheep men, but the lower country already had cattle in it, so they leased the backcountry to the sheep men. They sent thousands of sheep into the Dry Fork of the Blackfoot River and right into the heart of grizzly country. Them sheep men had a one-track mind—the only good bear was a dead one. I guess you couldn't blame them. They were only trying to make a living. My biggest beef was with the forest service for allowing sheep into that country in the first place.

These sheep men would hire a guy to cut trails for the sheep and shoot bears. This man would carry a bottle of strychnine with him and when he found a sheep or deer, or any other dead animal, he'd poison the meat. It didn't matter whether a grizzly did the killing or not.

Every bear in the area was wiped out, and so was every wolf and coyote, and all the furbearers like Canadian lynx and marten. I was trapping back in those days, running long wilderness traplines on snowshoes during the winter, and the strychnine was killing off every living thing that ate meat. For a while there everybody was carrying strychnine, even lots of the old outfitters. They'd have their guides sprinkle the poison on the gut pile of any animal their clients killed. It just seemed to me to be such an evil thing, that strychnine, and such an unnatural way for the men who supposedly loved the wild free life to respond. I argued with them over it many times. I got through some of their thick skulls that they were actually poisoning themselves by killing the game that supported them. That was during the time when a lot of clients were showing up, asking to hunt bull elk and maybe see a grizzly. That really turned the outfitters' heads, and a lot of them quit shooting and poisoning the bears.

Eventually, the forest service stopped leasing sheep range in the area, and with fewer outfitters prone to shoot every bear on sight, more and more grizzlies were seen in the Bob. But old habits die hard, even among government men. Howard explained:

Back in the late 1950s after the sheep men were gone, the grizzly really started coming back. This ranger from the Seeley Lake Ranger District asked me to keep track of the grizzlies and pinpoint their whereabouts on a map. In late August I handed the ranger a map with thirty-six marks on it—one for every bear I saw. I felt real good about what I'd done, figuring they'd be protecting those bears. That fall during hunting season I rode into a hunting camp, and these guys tell me they're hunting grizzly bears and show me a map. It was an exact copy of my map, with the bear locations penciled in. From that day on, I've refused to aid the forest service or the state in any grizzly mapping.

Though Howard admired the grizzly for its power and fearlessness, he was also a realist about the bear's temperament. "About the time you start thinking of a grizzly as man's friend, you're headed for trouble," he said. "They're not like us. They don't like this one or that one. They just want to be left alone. I've seen enough of the bad side of the bear that I don't trust them. And if you spend enough time in grizzly country, you'll eventually see the bad side of the bear."

"Like the bear that treed you?" I asked.

Howard nodded and exclaimed, "Oh, that was the meanest bear I ever met!"

Howard's ordeal began inauspiciously, like most grizzly encounters. One of his hunting clients had harvested a bull elk the evening before in Hay Creek. That fall had been a poor one for bear food. The berry crop had failed, and black bears and grizzlies were much in evidence as they ranged extensively in search of food before hibernation.

The next morning Howard rode his horse and two pack mules up a ridge cloaked in lodgepole pine toward the elk carcass. Dense barricades of blown-down trees halted the horse. Howard had noticed black bear tracks in the snow, and when he arrived at the spot where the elk was supposed to be, he found only skid marks where a bear had dragged off the carcass.

All I had with me was a little 25-35 saddle rifle. All those war injuries played havoc on my legs and hip, so I got in the habit of carrying that little gun to cut down on the weight. I followed the drag trail into a spruce thicket and slipped forward, with the intention of putting a bullet behind the bear's ear. I could hear the bear just ahead, so I bent low under some spruce branches. The hair stood up on the back of my neck when I looked right into the eyes of a big grizzly not 30 feet away. That grizzly didn't know where I was at that point, but he knew something was up. He stood on his hind legs and his silver-tipped mane was all puffed out, and he was bellowing and sniffing the air. No way I was going to try shooting a grizzly with that little gun, so I started backing out of there, but the bear heard me and here he come.

Like I told you, I barely made it up a tree ahead of him. I knew I was in a tight spot. I was maybe 30 yards from the bear's cache, and I knew my brother, Wendel, would be coming looking for me, and he'd walk right into that bear. I figured I had to do something, so I hatched the plan to wait until the bear settled down and then try to get to another tree until I got far enough away that the bear would leave me alone.

I clung to that skinny lodgepole pine tree for an hour before the bear finally curled up and dropped his head. I started easing down the tree, but the bear heard me and started bellowing and hit that tree so hard it almost knocked me out of it. I waited another hour, and this time I made it to the ground before the bear come after me. It was close, but I made it up another lodgepole just ahead of the bear. Oh, he was mad! He tore up the ground and bit that tree and swatted at it. Then he went back to the elk carcass. I gave it another hour and when I hit the ground again the bear was after me. By then I was about 60 yards away, and I figured maybe one more tree and that ol' bear would leave me alone.

Sure enough, I hit the ground and run to another tree and climbed it, and when I looked back, the griz was standing at the edge of the thicket watching me, but he hadn't come on the run. I give it only about fifteen minutes the next time before I slipped down to the ground, when I looked back, the bear was still in the thicket, so I was able to slip away.

Oh man, I was dragged out when I finally made it back to camp in the dark. I told my story to Wendel and the other boys, and I expected them to feel really sorry for me. Instead, they started laughing! They thought my almost getting bit by that bear was funny. I don't know if I was madder at the griz or at them.

Howard blamed himself for that bear incident. "It was all my fault," he said. "When I saw those black bear tracks in the snow, I just took it for granted that it was the same black bear that had dragged off the elk. I never bothered to look closer at the bear tracks. But sometimes with a grizzly, you don't have to do anything wrong. Sometimes it's just a matter of being in the wrong place at the wrong time."

That's exactly what occurred one fall as Howard was leading two elk hunters on horseback along a ridge of dense lodgepole pine on the west side of Danaher Pass. The trees became too thick for the horses, so the men dismounted and continued quietly on foot.

I was in the lead, searching the forest below for elk, when this big bellow comes from right behind me and here comes this grizzly charging out of the lodgepole at me. I dodged him and took off back to the two hunters because they had guns. You should have seen their eyes when I ran past them yelling, "Shoot! Shoot the bear!" Both men started firing and they emptied their guns at the grizzly as it chased me. Them guys never touched that bear with a bullet, but all the noise scared it away. As we continued up the ridge, we cut another smaller bear track, and I think that the smaller bear had been harassing the bigger bear, and it had charged me thinking I was the small bear.

Howard was not a trained wildlife biologist, but he had strong opinions about grizzly behavior that are seldom shared in professional circles. What he knew about the bear came from hundreds of hours of sitting back and watching them. Through the years Howard said he'd watched maybe 200 grizzlies while they were unaware of his presence. "I think that some of the bigger bears are treated with reverence and respect by other bears," he said. "Three times I've found where a dead bear had been buried by another bear, with its head sticking above the ground. The first time I found such a thing, I thought a human had done it, but there was just bear tracks on the grave. I know it sounds crazy, but I saw what I saw."

Another behavioral trait of the grizzly that amazed Howard was the great bear's cunning.

> I've seen where the bigger grizzlies will hunt bull elk during the rut by sneaking in close to a rutting bull, then grunting like they were another elk in rut. Then when the real bull comes looking for his competitor, the grizzly pounces on him. I've found several mature bull elk dead in dense thickets on Whiskey Ridge and Cabin Creek in the Bob. Their necks had been broken and big bear tracks were everywhere. Years ago I read a magazine article about a bear researcher who'd observed a grizzly doing the same thing in the Pelican Valley in Yellowstone. Some guys might laugh, but it's a proven fact that the grizzlies have learned to associate a hunter's gunshots with a gut pile and come on the run, and many's the hunter who discovered a grizzly sneaking in on him while he's bugling at an elk.

Recent findings by scientists at the Amboseli Elephant Research Project in Tsavo, Kenya, lend credence to Howard's claim about grizzly vocalizings. An elephant named Mlaika astounded researchers when she began closely imitating the sounds of trucks passing by on a nearby highway. Dr. Peter Tyack said, "These findings electrified me. Birds, bats, dolphins, and whales mimic sounds, but learning of a whole new animal group capable of vocal learning is fascinating."

And while Howard agreed that a grizzly can be dangerous under the wrong conditions, he also maintained that the animals mostly want to be left alone to enjoy life. He said that play, even among older bears, is common.

> One time I was leading a client up the east side of the Mission Mountains and we saw this big grizzly standing above a long snow chute just under McDonald Peak. That snow chute was almost straight up and down, and the bear

suddenly jumps into it. Pretty soon he's sailing down at probably 30 miles an hour, sitting on his haunches and bellowing like crazy. I figure the bear's trying to commit suicide because there's nothing but huge boulders below. But when the bear gets to the bottom of the snow chute it takes a great leap and lands on a big boulder and continues hopping from boulder to boulder until it can stop. That bear turned around and trudged up that snow chute and again we watched it slide down, bellowing as it went.

The power of the great bear never ceased to amaze Howard. "You should see one digging for marmots," he said. "There's dirt and rocks flying everywhere! They'll move 3 yards of dirt in ten minutes and dig a hole 5 feet deep to get at a marmot. I've also seen bears roll back boulders 500 pounds or more to get at the grubs underneath. Couple times me and other guys tried to roll the boulders back in place and we couldn't even budge them."

Another thing that grizzlies do, Howard said, is pack animals on their backs like men. He recalled a time he was guiding an elk hunter and they sneaked up to a water hole and found a dead mule deer buck that a grizzly had just killed. "There was fresh snow, and we saw where the grizzly had walked off. We came back a half hour later and the mule deer was gone, but there was no skid trail. That bear had grabbed the big mule deer that musta weighed 250 pounds and slung it over its back, then walked off."

Howard remembered another time when game warden Bruce Neal responded to outfitter Gordon Bill's complaint about a grizzly raiding his hunting camp. Bill had an old mule that had gone lame with arthritis, so he took it out and shot it. The warden gave one of the hunting clients a grizzly tag, and both men settled back to wait for the big bear. They were lounging a half hour later when a huge grizzly later estimated to weigh 800 pounds thundered out of the forest, grabbed the 1,000-pound mule carcass and threw the animal into the air and body slammed it. The hunter forgot about shooting and jumped up and yelled, "Look at that!" Whereupon the bear grabbed the mule, threw it over its back and retreated into the timber.

Howard disagreed with outfitters who want to shoot every bear that raids a camp.

> We're invading their homes with all these tasty smells. What do we expect when a grizzly comes wandering into camp? Through the years, ol' Slewfoot raided my camps about forty times. I never even thought of shooting him. He got to be such a frequent visitor at some of my camps that the horses, usually terrified when a grizzly comes near, didn't even bother to raise a ruckus. I remember one time I went out to the corral and found the horses munching hay on one side of the rail fence, with Slewfoot not 10 feet away eating grain from a bucket.
>
> All those years being around my camp, I had no trouble with Slewfoot. Fact is, he became quite a draw for the hunters to see a real grizzly. But then Slewfoot started getting mean. He was twenty-six years old and having some trouble walking with that bad foot. I think it made him mean. He started chasing horses and riders he met on the trail. In a couple of my camps he chased the hunters when they were headed for the privy. I knew something had to be done, or we were going to end up with a dead hunter.

This was back in 1972 when it was still legal to still hunt grizzlies in Montana, so Howard bought a bear permit. In the meantime Slewfoot had raided another camp and devoured three bags of oats weighing 300 pounds. "I followed Slewfoot's tracks to a willow thicket," Howard said with a wicked grin. "You never seen such a mess. Slewfoot got diarrhea, and there was a half-acre patch of willow flattened and oats sprayed everywhere. That bear musta been in torment."

After Slewfoot raided another camp three nights in a row, Howard and his son, Steve, arrived at sundown and sat in the open horse tent waiting for the bear. Within minutes he showed up, and as soon as

Howard saw the bruin, he knew things had changed. "Ol' Slewfoot had always been amiable, but the look in that bear's eyes was murderous. As soon as he saw us he charged. Steve had a big gun, a .338 magnum, and he emptied it into the bear, but it kept coming."

The only thing standing between the two men and the bellowing grizzly closing in on them was Howard's lever-action 30-30 carbine. "I didn't have time to aim. I just started shooting from the hip like *The Rifleman* [a popular TV western featuring Chuck Connors]. Slewfoot nosedived just 10 feet from me. When we skinned out the carcass, we discovered that the bear had suffered a slashing wound to its leg that had turned it inward, probably from a big boar, when it was a cub."

The subject of hunting grizzlies has always drawn heated arguments. The grizzly has not been hunted south of the Canadian border since 1976, when it was placed on the Endangered Species List. Until then, Montana issued about a dozen grizzly hunting permits, mostly in the wilderness areas and national forests adjacent to Glacier National Park, to harvest surplus bears. However, some people, like Howard Copenhaver, believe that it's time to again allow limited grizzly hunting as a management tool to remove problem bears.

> I think hunting the grizzly is the best way to keep them wary of man and make them stay back in their wilderness haunts. Bears don't like humans, and if we don't put the fear of man into them, they become brazen. Look at what that lady [Carrie Hunt] is doing with her bear dogs and rubber bullets to problem bears. She's putting the fear of man back into those bears.
>
> There's way more bears now than back in the 1950s. I wouldn't even hazard a guess on how many grizzlies are in the Bob, but it's got to be more than one hundred. Last year on a pack trip into the Bob, I saw an average of three grizzlies each day. That's just too many bears. Some of these are getting chased out of the country by bigger bears, and they're ending up as problem bears that we're spending thousands of dollars to live trap a couple times,

then some state game warden ends up shooting them anyway. We could sell grizzly permits for $10,000 and use that money to move some of the bears into the Bitterroots. I guarantee you, those permits would be snapped up. We could have a state game warden take the hunter out to where a problem bear is hanging out and have the hunter take it out of the system. What's so wrong with that? People think if we just let the grizzly keep multiplying it'll take over all its former range, but mostly it's million dollar homes there now. The bears just get into trouble, scare people, and they get killed anyway.

In his later years Howard turned most of his outfitting operation over to his son, Steve. He became more interested in mentoring the new breed of outdoorsmen entering the wilderness. "Most of 'em were dudes. They grew up in the city and got all their learning from books. They were walking hazards to themselves and the animals."

Will Kats readily admits that the day he and his dog met Howard on a narrow trail in the North Forth of the Blackfoot River, he was in dire need of mentoring.

I'm sure I was quite a sight to Howard. I'd been living in the woods all year. My hair was long, and I carried a huge assortment of ragged homemade gear. I stepped off the trail and we hailed each other. Howard suddenly stopped and said, "Hey, you wouldn't happen to have a cigarette, would you?" I gave him a paper and can of loose tobacco. While he rolled a smoke, he asked where I was headed.

"I'm headed up the Danaher to trap marten," I said.

"Are ya now?" Howard replied. "Got a good rain outfit and some pitch wood to start a fire in wet weather?"

"Uh, no," I replied.

"How about a hatchet?"

"It's in my dog's pack," I mumbled.

"How about scissors? You got any scissors?"

"Uh, no," I replied. "What would I need scissors for?"

"Well, for starters, you could cut that hair of yours."

Then he rode off. Howard was never one to mince words. But we met again, and that's when my education began—about wolverines, and the best ridges to trap marten, and elk wallows and grizzly bears, and how to live off the land, and the beauty of God's natural world.

Will Kats is just one of hundreds of men whose lives were changed by Howard Copenhaver. Many the wealthy client showed up for an elk hunt with a fat wallet and an attitude but after a dose of Howard's wisdom and backcountry wilderness tutoring returned to the corporate world with a newly acquired sense of humility.

Beside his great humanitarian effort, Howard also had a huge impact on the welfare of the grizzly bear because of his strident support for the great bear back in the days when its foothold beyond Glacier was tenuous. Bear experts now point out that a bear movement corridor between the stable grizzly populations in Yellowstone and Glacier is critical to the continued survival of the great bear. This corridor is comprised of a vast north-south ridge system, with the Swan Mountains on the west side, where Bud Cheff preaches temperance toward the grizzly, and the Bob Marshall and Scapegoat Wilderness Areas to the east, where Howard Copenhaver delivered a similar message. To the south this corridor funnels into the vast Bitterroot Range, where Bud Moore continues to speak out for the reintroduction of the great bear.

Howard Copenhaver's name, like that of Bud Cheff and Bud Moore, is little known in today's high-profile world of eco-bear warriors, but to wildlife biologists and bear experts, his contributions to the ultimate success of the grizzly bear are considered priceless. Howard literally stood in the gap for the grizzly at a time when hate and fear, and bullets and strychnine, threatened to extinguish its spirit from the land.

CHAPTER 6

⊹•≫≪•⊹•≫≪•⊹•≫≪•⊹

JOHN AND FRANK CRAIGHEAD

PIONEERING MODERN BEAR BIOLOGY

"My God, I'd never seen anything like it," John Craighead effused as we sat at his kitchen table in his Missoula, Montana, home on a late October evening in 2004. [John's twin brother Frank Craighead passed away in 2001 in Moose, Wyoming, not far from the Teton Mountains.] "Frank and I had seen plenty of beautiful mountains in Pennsylvania, but the day our old '28 Chevy topped this hill in Wyoming and we spotted the Tetons [Grand Teton National Park], it was like our souls got sucked right into the Rocky Mountains. We knew right then and there that our calling was out West, and that any professional endeavor would have to somehow be centered in those mountains."

If the Craighead brothers were primed for the Rocky Mountains, so also were the Rockies awaiting them. For deep within the bosom of this great mass of rock and forest lumbered a surly beast that asked no quarter and gave none. Its strength and cunning were already legend long before the Craigheads topped that rise in the foothills of the Tetons, but this great and horrible beast we call the grizzly bear was in grave need of help, having been besieged for more than a century by fear, hate, and an ignorance of its ways. What possible good could two eastern boys from, God forbid, Washington, D.C., hope to accomplish? As it turned out, plenty. The Craighead brothers were more than up to the task. They brought to life the grizzly bear for the modern scientific world. And they brought the great bear charging into our living rooms via television, thereby creating an instant nationwide enthusiasm for the animal.

John and Frank had been nature boys since their early days growing up in Washington, D.C. Though their home and family were definitely upper middle class, the two Craighead boys could always be found in the woods, studying frogs and snails and fish and birds. When it came time for college, they enrolled at Pennsylvania State University. "They didn't have any wildlife programs in any of the colleges at the time," John told me. "Frank and I chose biology as our major. Exactly what that meant as far as a career went, we didn't know."

During that time both young men wrestled at the collegiate level, developing their upper body strength. They didn't know it at the time, but even their sport was preparing them for their careers, especially when they were forced to hastily climb a tree to avoid a confrontation with a grizzly.

Frank and John enrolled in the University of Michigan's post-graduate biology program, and while there, began teaching an outdoor training course for surveyors and foresters. "After World War Two broke out," John reminisced, "the Navy asked us to teach a survival course to their naval pilots and marines. Our first course was at Chapel Hill, and we were teaching a bunch of tough marines. The first thing we wanted them to do was climb a palm tree and bring down a coconut. Me and Frank scooted right up a tree, but the marines couldn't do it and complained they were being trained by a bunch of monkeys."

After the war, the Craigheads continued their studies. Frank found work as a professor in the Environmental Research Institute at the State University of New York. John joined the Montana Wildlife Cooperative Wildlife Research Unit at the University of Montana. While there, he began reading up on the grizzly, Montana's state animal and the symbol of all that was still wild and free in the West. John recalled:

> It was a short read. There was almost nothing scientific to
> study about the grizzly. Adolph Murie had studied

grizzlies in Alaska, and there was a book by Enos Mills, but it was mostly behavioral stuff and nothing you'd call scientific. Enos Mills's book was so old that he had thirteen different scientific classifications for the grizzly.

Frank and I decided to study the grizzly scientifically. Our main goal was to analyze the grizzly's reproductive rate and all the science surrounding it, and the mortality rate to see exactly how the grizzly population was faring. If the mortality rate was higher than the reproductive rate, then the grizzly was in danger of vanishing, and vice versa. We put together a program and got the funding for it. We looked all over the West and finally chose Yellowstone because that was where the greatest concentrations of grizzlies could be found in the lower states. We were also aware that the park had been feeding their grizzlies garbage behind their hotels, and we thought those bears would be much more visible and easy to gain scientific information on. I wasn't real happy to be studying bears that frequented dumps and would've preferred something in the heart of the wilderness. One thing we learned was that as soon as those bears left the dump, they acted like any wild grizzly.

Yellowstone Park in 1959 had all the trappings of a modern park, with up-to-date facilities and multiple paved roads to handle the millions of tourists visiting annually. However, its bear management was still primitive. Essentially, park rangers dealt with black and grizzly bears only when they had a problem with them. If a bear attacked someone or if it began breaking into facilities or became a pest or a danger in a campground, it was either relocated, shipped off to a zoo, or killed. The park had no idea how many grizzlies it had and had not even attempted a count in the nine years prior to the Craigheads' arrival.

The Craigheads began a vigorous program of live-trapping grizzlies, using either culvert traps or a CO_2-powered dart gun to sedate free-roaming animals. After a grizzly was immobilized (conscious, but unable to move), it was weighed and measured. A blood sample was drawn, and a tooth extracted to discern its age. Colored ear tags were fastened to females, and males received aluminum ear tags. Females with young were especially attractive to the researchers as they tackled the monumental task of gathering reproductive data.

During these early years the Craighead brothers could best be described as whirling dervishes—constantly on the move as they grunted and hoisted sedated grizzly bears onto scales or stalked close enough to put a tranquilizing dart into a bear's butt. (During the twelve-year study period, 389 grizzlies were tagged and studied.) They also followed ear-tagged bears for miles into the wilderness, gathering information about their reproductive, feeding, denning, and mortality cycles. This early period was a time of cordial relations and cooperation between the researchers and park managers, and the Craigheads often assisted rangers in live-trapping problem bears.

Data began to accumulate, and though the Craigheads were far too professional to begin drawing conclusions from a few seasons' findings, certain tendencies were already becoming apparent: A lot of young bears were dying inside the park, and a lot of big bears were dying outside of it. As a result the Craigheads felt impelled to study intensely the reproductive-versus-mortality dynamics of Yellowstone's grizzlies. And a lot of it was at close range.

"We climbed into many a bear's den to see what it was like," John explained. "A lot of these were narrow tunnels leading to a bigger chamber at the end." John rubbed the nape of his neck and added with a wry grin:

> The hair would raise up on the back of my neck as I crawled back there to have a look. The bears aren't supposed to be there in the summer, but it was always a relief when the flashlight shone on an empty den. We also found that some grizzlies were a lot more social than we were led to believe. I remember two females, I think they

Frank and John Craighead with radio-tracking
devices on Dunraven Pass

FRANK CRAIGHEAD COLLECTION

were [ear tag] numbers 98 and 101. These sows had cubs; and they not only hung around and fed with each other during the summer, but they even denned close to each other. Grizzlies like to den in the same area every year where they feel secure, and they'll use the same den year after year if at all possible. They line their winter dens with grass and conifer boughs.

On the subject of danger, John shrugged and said:

If we thought a situation might be dangerous, we'd carry a sawed-off shotgun loaded with buckshot. We probably had a couple thousand grizzly encounters in the twelve years we were in Yellowstone, and we never came close to

111

using that shotgun on a bear. I think twice we climbed trees to avoid a confrontation with an aggressive bear, but we were good at it [climbing trees], so it never got out of hand. A couple times I walked around a tree and surprised a sleeping grizzly. They huffed and popped their teeth, but they prefer to avoid a man and they moved off.

I just feel that if you know grizzly behavior, and you make some noise to let them know you're coming, they'll move off. Many times during our studies we moved in on radio-collared bears in their day beds. We knew exactly where they were located, but when we got there, the bear had heard or smelled us and was gone. I don't think people who travel in grizzly country have any idea how many bears they make contact without ever knowing about it. Even sows with cubs, and they're the most aggressive.

One of the best illustrations of how distance and human noise can neutralize a tense situation with a grizzly was noted in a Craighead research paper on grizzly-human relationships. One fall, John and Frank were radio-tracking a 450-pound female with two yearling cubs in the 250-pound range. The men were particularly concerned that this sow, being a particularly aggressive bear in the past, might charge if surprised. Even though the men were being careful and continually monitoring the sow's location with the receiver, they inadvertently found themselves within 100 feet of the bears, which had bedded in a dense stand of lodgepole pine and blown-down trees. Fortunately, their scent was being carried away from the bears, so the brothers silently retreated about 100 yards and climbed trees. Then they deliberately began talking loudly. The female bellowed and all three bears charged about 30 yards to see if the source of danger was anywhere close, then they galloped off. John explained:

> The big boars get testy during mating season, but we found the females day in and day out to be a lot more aggressive than the males. The one thing that Frank and I

always kept in mind was that the grizzly is unpredictable, so we tried to avoid getting ourselves into a predicament that might force a bear to react differently from what we expected. More than once, we climbed trees when we thought we might be too close to a bear in thick cover. We weren't scared; it was just a safety thing. Of course, we never left food around camp. That's just inviting trouble in grizzly country.

One of the more ominous findings of the Craighead team involved the danger of the wild grizzly becoming conditioned to the presence of man. Usually this was the result of a food reward. The Craigheads called such bears "food-conditioned." In later years, wildlife biologists would coin the term "habituation" to describe a bear that has lost its natural fear of people, almost always leading to aggression, injury, or death to bear and human alike.

The Craigheads cited an example of a forest survey crew working in a remote area of Mount Washburn, miles from any development. When the three crew members first encountered a three-year-old grizzly of about 250 pounds, the bear reacted as expected, running off and avoiding the area where the men were working. Over the next few weeks, the bear began rummaging through the area after the men had returned to their camp or civilization on the weekend. The men had fallen into the habit of burying their lunch trash in a shallow depression or under a rock, and the bear began digging up this food.

At first the men were thrilled when the bear, rather than bounding off at their presence, began to approach them, timidly at first, and was rewarded with lunch scraps thrown to him. The bear quickly became bolder, and when no food scraps were made available, he began making bluff charges. Five times the young grizzly treed the crew members and then rifled through their packs and lunch pails.

In just two weeks, this bear's personality had changed from timid and retiring to unpredictable and dangerous—all because of a few food handouts. The bear ultimately became so disruptive that the Craigheads were asked to immobilize the animal, but after hiking into the area, they could not locate him. The following day a male grizzly matching the bear's description appeared at the Canyon Village campground. The Craigheads captured the bear and applied tag no. 80 to its right ear. Eleven days later the tagged grizzly was recaptured at the Indian Creek Campground 7 miles away and released in a remote section of the park, 30 air miles from any developments.

Nothing more was heard from this bear for more than a year, after which time park rangers killed it. The bear's fatal mistake was harassing campers in a wilderness area near Lewis Lake. The Craigheads point to this bear as a prime example of the tragic results of even very limited food handouts.

Since this was the first truly scientific study of the grizzly bear, the Craigheads would undoubtedly have gained recognition among wildlife biologists in succeeding years. However, John and Frank Craighead would not only be recognized but would become folk heroes thanks to the black-and-white television sets rapidly filling living rooms throughout the country.

One of the Craigheads' sponsors, The National Geographic Society, had already begun filming nature programs for the new television market. However, movie cameras in the early 1960s were cumbersome and heavy, making any filming in the field difficult. But in Yellowstone, National Geographic was aware of the potential of filming the normally reclusive grizzly as it came and went to garbage dumps. National Geographic received permission from the park service and the Craigheads to tag along with the researchers as they went about trapping, tagging, and following bears.

National Geographic programs featuring the Craighead brothers manhandling the powerful grizzly became instant hits. Families all across the country sat glued to their TVs watching the robust nature boys go about their business of gaining data. The most memorable incident of the entire National Geographic venture occurred while John and Frank were working on a large, immobilized male grizzly. The animal had already been weighed and given an antidote to speed its recovery from the sedative. Frank and John believed they had plenty of time to gather their gear and be gone before the bear again became dangerous, but the grizzly was already showing signs of recovery. And the signs weren't good. Whenever the bear moved a paw or reared its head, it was directed at the men. At one point it half-lunged at John before crumpling to the ground. The men began frantically gathering their valuable equipment, but when the bear suddenly rose to its haunches, all was forgotten. John and Frank took off running toward their vehicle parked about 60 yards away.

I remember sitting on the edge of my chair in the living room of my home in northeastern Pennsylvania and watching the episode unfold. While the Craigheads sprinted for the vehicle, the grizzly stood. It had many directions it could turn to escape. But from the look on that bear's face, it had revenge, not escape, on its mind.

The bear stood wobbly-legged for a second before charging after the men in a comical lilting gallop. But even a drugged bear can outrun a man. The grizzly was gaining fast when the Craigheads dove into the vehicle's cab. Everyone—including the National Geographic cameraman, the Craigheads, and myself—thought the incident was over. But not the grizzly. Instead of veering off, the bear gained momentum as it approached the pickup. Gone was its slapstick drunken gait, replaced suddenly by a furious, focused rush. A second later 800 pounds of grizzly slammed into the pickup door. The bear staggered backwards onto its haunches, leaving a 3-foot dent in the heavy steel door. The grizzly then got to its feet and galloped into the forest.

As a result of this television exposure, John and Frank Craighead became the first true outdoor personalities, beating by several years the venerable Marlin Perkins of "Mutual of Omaha's Wild Kingdom." The media exposure was nice, but the men were, first and foremost, scientists. Though they attended various functions during the off-season, they remained focused on their studies in Yellowstone.

However, the research team was often frustrated by its inability to stay with some tagged bears. The grizzly roamed so extensively at times that even the toughest man could not keep up. In addition, bears were often lost in dense forest. That all changed in the summer of 1962, when the Craigheads began using a radio-tracking system to locate bears. This system had been developed by Frank Craighead and his son in the summer of 1961 and perfected over the winter. Specifically, a sedated bear was fitted with a neck collar containing a radio transmitter. A hand-held receiver tuned to that particular transmitter's frequency allowed researchers to quickly and accurately pinpoint the bear's location, day or night, summer or winter. A total of forty-eight radio transmitters were used on twenty-three different bears during the study. During the latter part of their work, the Craigheads began using microchip transmitters and satellites to track bears twenty-four hours per day.

This radio-tracking system is essentially the same method used by researchers today. Around the world, the most prestigious wildlife researchers point to the Craigheads' invention as the single most important tool ever developed for studying wildlife. In fact immediately following the Yellowstone bear study, John Craighead flew to Africa and helped scientists implant microchips in the horns of the endangered white rhinoceros to stave off its extinction.

Beginning in 1962 and continuing in a series of scientific papers, the Craigheads stayed true to their initial goal of monitoring reproductive and mortality rates. What they found was both intriguing and startling. Females did not successfully mate until four years of age, and only every two to three years after that. An average of just two cubs was born, and fewer than half (47 percent) survived through their second year.

Throughout the 1960s grizzly-bear hunting was still legal. Montana allowed fall hunting by permit, and Wyoming allowed both spring and fall hunting and even baiting. The Craigheads' research found that 47 percent of all bear mortality was due to hunters who killed grizzlies that strayed beyond park boundaries. That, coupled with other bear mortality within the park from accidents and predation and the removal of problem bears by rangers, placed the average yearly mortality rate equal to the existing reproductive rate.

Yellowstone's grizzly population wasn't dwindling, but neither was it growing. "We looked at it this way," John said, and pointed a gnarled index finger into the air to stress his point. "We didn't have much control over the birth rate, but we did have some control over the death rate. We felt there were just way too many bears being killed outside the park."

The researchers were concerned that it wouldn't take much of a fluctuation in these dynamics to tip the scales toward the great bear's decline, putting its continued survival in danger. That danger would soon present itself in the form of a radical policy change by the National Park Service concerning its garbage dumps.

The friendly air of cooperation between researchers and park managers had slowly deteriorated over the years as the Craigheads received more and more media attention, even while the park had brought in its own wildlife biologists, who felt they were being left out of the more glamorous grizzly-bear research.

Adding to this festering rivalry was a growing sentiment within the National Park Service to close all garbage dumps and return the national parks to as near-natural conditions as possible.

Paul Schullery, in his book *The Bears of Yellowstone,* goes into detail about the rivalry and the dump closure debate between the Craigheads and the park service. Schullery's book takes on a decidedly pro–park-service flavor, but it should be remembered that Schullery was employed by Yellowstone National Park when he wrote the book. Schullery specifically cites the Craigheads' 1967 report titled *Management of Bears in Yellowstone* as a document containing written proof the Craigheads were against closing the dumps all at once. The brothers advised a gradual closing to avoid potential harm to the existing grizzly population, which at the time was estimated at about 170 bears.

I obtained a copy of this report. On page 93 is a section titled, "Elimination of Refuse Dumps," in which the Craigheads wrote:

> The unsightly and "unnatural" refuse dumps that have
> existed for so long in Yellowstone are not in keeping with

national park scenic standards or philosophy. Although the dumps where grizzlies feed are not often visited by the public, they are frequently viewed by dignitaries and scholars of our own and foreign countries who wish to obtain a first look at a grizzly bear. The experience of viewing a grizzly under such conditions, though interesting and even thrilling, does not enhance the image of either the park service or the grizzly.

However, concentration of grizzlies during the summer at refuse dumps has both advantages and disadvantages in the management of the species. Forty-three percent of all grizzly deaths occur when they move out of the park sanctuary and are shot by hunters. Since the refuse dumps within the park attract and hold grizzlies for extended periods of time, they reduce outward movement in summer and fall and by so doing lower the mortality.

The report agreed with the park service that there was sufficient natural food in the park to sustain the existing grizzly population, but warned that since 92 percent of the park's grizzlies visited the dumps, they would need time to learn new foraging techniques; a gradual phasing out of the dumps would allow bears to supplement their diminishing food supply at the dumps with natural foods.

The Craigheads' main criticism of the abrupt dump closure was that it might cause bears to begin roaming far beyond park boundaries, getting into trouble at ranches and campgrounds. But the greatest danger to the bears came from hunters. And it should be remembered that even with the dumps in operation, hunters waiting beyond park boundaries killed 47 percent of the bears. What would happen when an unprecedented wave of hungry bears wandered beyond park boundaries? The park service refused to address any problems that might occur beyond its borders, even if the animals being killed were park grizzlies. On page 103 of the report, the Craigheads suggested that a 10-mile buffer zone extending beyond the boundary of the park, consisting of approximately 2,000 square miles, be closed to grizzly hunting. This would eliminate almost entirely the problem of park bears being shot as soon as they stepped beyond the boundary line.

Yellowstone's Chief Biologist Glen Cole, ignoring the significant mortality rate of bears that wandered outside the park, stated he was uncomfortable with the report's lack of concrete scientific data to support their opinions. However, the park service's main dislike for this report may instead have been the Craigheads' summation of the park service's current wildlife conservation programs, which were almost nonexistent. On page 80, the Craigheads summed up their views: "No integrated plan exists for managing the grizzly throughout Yellowstone National Park and adjacent forest areas." While the report was scientifically accurate and not intended as a condemnation, park service managers seethed over what they felt was open criticism. Yet, in the exhaustive text preceding this statement, the Craigheads laid out their areas of concern, ranging from the problem of managing the overpopulation of elk and bison in the park, to the absence of a viable plan for grizzly-bear management by the park service if the dumps were closed immediately.

Resentment festered to the point where neither side was communicating with the other except by letter. This squabble-turned-feud escalated in 1969, prompting the secretary of the interior to send investigators from the Natural Science Advisory Committee to Yellowstone to hear both sides of the dump issue. The Craigheads presented their recommendations in a two-hour session, but only after all park personnel left the room. The advisory committee reluctantly agreed with the Craigheads to a slow phasing out of the dumps. However, after complaints by the park service that the "slow closure" program was not working, all park dumps were closed.

Garbage from residences, restaurants, and hotels within the park was trucked outside park boundaries, leaving the bears, accustomed to a steady diet of human food, with "nothing" to eat because they were not accustomed to foraging for natural food. The bears dispersed, as park officials had hoped, but not to seek wilderness food sources. Instead, bears continued to satiate their craving for human food by tearing apart garbage cans behind restaurants, or tearing off doors to help themselves inside.

And then the killings began. In 1970 Yellowstone National Park rangers killed twelve grizzlies and sent eight others to zoos. That same year, twenty-four more bears were known to have died, either from management actions or illegal and legal kills in neighboring states. In 1971 the park admitted to killing eight grizzlies and sending one to a zoo, but kills in neighboring states brought the count up to forty-four. In the first two years after the dumps were close, eighty-eight grizzlies had been killed—an enormous loss for a population estimated by the Craigheads to be no more than 170 to 180 bears.

The killings continued in 1972, though at a lower rate. Twenty-four grizzlies perished that year. In 1973 eighteen bears were killed, and in 1974 sixteen more were eliminated. The park service cited this reduced figure as proof that the closing of the dumps, after an initial spike in grizzly deaths, had indeed leveled off. Critics screamed that the lower kill numbers from 1973 to 1975 were a result of a grizzly population decimated by the carnage of the first two years! Some biologists estimate that in 1975 the grizzly population within the park may have dipped to as low as forty individuals.

Rumors and thinly veiled accusations from Craighead supporters continued through those contentious years of 1972 to 1975. One of the most persistent rumors was that park rangers were killing far more problem bears and not reporting them. Accusations of massive clandestine killings of problem grizzly bears by park rangers were common fodder for newspapers. In his book, Schullery discounts such accusations, saying that he was employed by the park at the time and saw no proof of such grizzly killings. In addition, he said, there were so many people traveling through every sector of the park that it would have been impossible for such grizzly killings to go undetected.

And then again, maybe not. In 1986 I wrote an article exposing the illegal killing of thirteen trophy bull elk by two hunters who had been sneaking into the backcountry south of Yellowstone's Mount

Washburn for four years. These men were caught when one of them poached a mule deer buck in Utah, and investigating wardens discovered a videotape showing the men killing the elk with Mount Washburn in the background.

Despite all the bitterness, the Craigheads were willing to shrug off their disagreements with park officials for the good of the great bear and science. They petitioned Yellowstone National Park to be allowed to do research on bears that roamed beyond the historic dump sites during the critical years of 1970 through 1975. Yellowstone officials, according to Schullery, did not want the Craigheads back in their park, but having taken a beating in the press, they were more careful in their response. They didn't say no, they just made demands that no researcher would accept. In a written statement, park officials stipulated that all oral and written statements, including press releases, had to be submitted first to officials. Second, all management activities and expressions of management of grizzly bears had to first be approved by the park service. The Craigheads, as the park service expected, declined, and as a result a potentially valuable research project was lost.

Dr. Chuck Jonkel (see chapter 7) told me, "What was done to the Craigheads by the park service ranks as one of the greatest outrages in wildlife biology. It wasn't just stupid. It was criminal."

One of the most important events during this dark period for the Yellowstone grizzly was the formation of the Interagency Grizzly Bear Study Team. The group consisted of research biologists from several federal and state wildlife agencies. After reviewing the data, this committee agreed with the Craigheads (Yellowstone Park officials continued to maintain the grizzly was not in danger) that the grizzly-bear population in the greater Yellowstone ecosystem had indeed been adversely impacted by the dump closures. Upon their recommendation the grizzly bear was classified as threatened on September 1, 1975, under the federal Endangered Species Act, which had been signed into law by President Richard Nixon earlier that year. Hunting grizzlies in Montana and Wyoming became illegal, thereby stanching the flow of grizzly blood at the park boundaries.

JOHN AND FRANK CRAIGHEAD

The 2005 grizzly population in the Yellowstone ecosystem is about 600 animals. The few park service supporters in the long-running controversy point to that number as vindication of the original Yellowstone forecast—an initial dip in grizzly numbers, followed by stability. However, most biologists point to the protection of the grizzly under the Endangered Species Act, and not park policy, as the essential factor in the tremendous growth in grizzly numbers over the next three decades.

With their study in Yellowstone completed, the Craigheads became strong advocates of wilderness, specifically those wildlands that could accommodate the grizzly. The brothers were convinced grizzly bears and people were not compatible and could not be next-door neighbors. If the grizzly was to be allowed to increase its numbers, appropriate habitat had to be identified and mapped.

John Craighead undertook the Herculean task of identifying and locating such places. Having previously discovered during his Yellowstone studies that grizzly habitat was tied to its never-ending search for food and isolation from man, John initiated an exhaustive study of seasonal grizzly food sources across the Northern Rockies. Through observations of bears, through track and scat analysis, he was able to pinpoint those areas and foods most preferred by the grizzly. Such areas were identified as *prime habitat.*

Using newly developed satellite imagery and computer analysis of data, he pinpointed the best habitat within a wilderness ecosystem, the places where a grizzly was most likely to flourish. His findings, published as *A Definitive System for Analysis of Grizzly Bear Habitat and Other Wilderness Resources,* have become an indispensable aid for wildlife managers as they seek suitable habitat for today's burgeoning grizzly population.

Hundreds of more recent grizzly-bear studies have appeared since John and Frank Craighead introduced modern grizzly-bear research in Yellowstone National Park. Today, thanks to the miracles of the cyber age, it's become a lot easier. A researcher can now sit in an air-conditioned office and connect his laptop to a satellite that monitors and gathers data on any number of grizzlies carrying microchip implants, roaming at that moment in the farthest corner of wilderness. Though such research projects usually garner useful bits of information, their cost is often prohibitive. Some biologists openly wonder if we haven't studied the grizzly to death—especially since the Craighead brothers furnished just about all we need to know to ensure the great bear's survival.

CHAPTER 7

┈┈╼╍╋╍╾┈┈╼╍╋╍╾┈┈╼╍╋╍╾┈┈

DR. CHUCK JONKEL

SAVING THE GRIZZLY
ALONG THE CANADIAN BORDER

Bowhunter Eric Burge hiked briskly up the trail toward the top of the mountain, spurred on by the musical bugling of rutting bull elk up ahead. The area he was hunting just north of Yellowstone National Park was famous for producing large bulls, but it was also known to harbor a healthy grizzly population, and Burge frankly had reservations about the ability of his newly purchased can of pepper spray to stop so formidable a beast.

As he approached a saddle, he spotted the top of a tan-colored animal coming over the crest. Elk! A jolt of adrenalin scorched his veins, but the excitement turned to shock when, instead of a bull elk, an enormous tan-colored sow grizzly with two large cubs ambled into view and started down the trail toward him. Burge stepped off the path and pulled the can of bear spray from its belt holster. The sow's head jerked up, eyes wide with surprise. The next instant she was in full charge with head down and ears laid back.

"This stuff better work," Burge thought as he raised the can of bear spray, "because she's not going to stop."

The onrushing sow was almost upon him when Burge shot an orange burst of bear spray into the bear's face. The sow skidded to a halt, flailed at the air and spun around twice before galloping down the trail with her two confused cubs trailing behind.

125

DR. CHUCK JONKEL

When I interviewed Burge six months later, he punctuated his story with the epithet, "That bear spray saved my life!"

"Actually," I corrected him, "Dr. Chuck Jonkel and Bill Pounds saved your life."

While I sat in a chair with 3-foot-high stacks of dust-covered documents on either side of me, watching Chuck Jonkel scatter papers around on his desk in the director's office of the Great Bear Foundation in Missoula, Montana, I had plenty of time to replay Eric Burge's bear-spray experience in my head and to study the man who helped, in cooperation with Bill Pounds, in its development.

Jonkel was searching for a copy of a letter he had recently sent to dozens of prominent wildlife biologists, urging them to step forward and be vocal in condemning the new wave of nature programs, which show people moving dangerously close to bears. After five minutes of searching, Jonkel finally slouched into his chair and commented, "I'll find that paper and send it to you."

Then, responding to my question about how he got started in bear research work, he replied, "I actually majored in geology because they didn't have any such thing as a wildlife majors in those days. But in my fourth year in college, they started a wildlife program, so I switched to it. Two weeks before graduation, a professor asked me if I wanted to enroll in a graduate program studying the pine marten, so I took the job. After my post-graduate work I took on a black-bear research job. That was back in 1958. Then I spent eight years studying the polar bear."

To put Chuck Jonkel's life in proper perspective, he had already completed his first bear research project before the Craighead brothers began their work in Yellowstone. The fact that Jonkel's work targeted the black and polar bears, rather than the grizzly, kept his name out of the headlines during the Craigheads' rise to fame in the early 1960s.

And Jonkel likes it that way. He's stayed out of the limelight during almost a half-century of bear research, preferring the environs of grizzly country to a padded seat in some antiseptic office or the podium at some glittery wildlife symposium. As a result his name is not a household word associated with the grizzly, yet his accomplishments in the understanding, management, and conservation of the grizzly rank right up there with the Craigheads'.

"My involvement with the grizzly began back in 1969 when I got a phone call from the state of Montana," he said. "They said they needed research on the grizzly along the border with Canada. I was looking for a job at the time, so I accepted the position of project coordinator. It was a ten-year project that started out well, but when the data started coming in, all hell broke loose."

The Border Grizzly Project's goal seemed harmless enough. Essentially, the purpose of the entire project was to fulfill a mandate of the Endangered Species Act (ESA) of 1973, which required every state and federal land agency not only to protect the grizzly bear but also to preserve and enhance its habitat. Though the grizzly had not yet been declared endangered, officials realized that listing was imminent. On September 1, 1975, the great bear was listed as "threatened" in accordance with the ESA.

The research team's goals were relatively simple. The first objective was to determine the status and future of the grizzly along Montana's border with Canada. Unlike the Yellowstone grizzly ecosystem, which is considered an island population because the bears are encircled by either unsuitable or off-limit habitat, the Border Grizzly Area is a vast tract of wildland beginning in the south at the Rattlesnake Wilderness just outside of Missoula, Montana, and running north through the Swan Mountains and the Bob Marshall Wilderness to the eastern front of the Rockies, then west all the way through the Selkirk Mountains of north Idaho and Eastern Washington and on to the northern Cascade Mountains. In the heart of the Border Grizzly Area are Glacier and Waterton National Parks and the adjoining areas of Alberta and British Columbia.

The second objective was to evaluate existing habitat and make recommendations for preserving and enhancing grizzly habitat. The research team was not required to gain data throughout this vast wilderness, only along the Montana border. Those findings could then be applied to the surrounding areas where applicable.

Dr. Chuck Jonkel with a bear skull

CENTER FOR WILDLIFE INFORMATION

Jonkel assembled an impressive corps of ambitious undergraduate and graduate students. He allowed them to pursue individual research projects that would count toward their graduate degrees as long as they were compatible with the goal of the project. The first full year of field work began in 1975. With great zeal the researchers spread out through the study area, live-trapping grizzlies using foot snares, tagging and radio-collaring bears, and monitoring their movements. Some students classified and evaluated grizzly habitat, while others studied the impacts on the grizzly of resource extraction activities such as logging and mining.

That first full year of work was exceptional for two reasons. First, a tremendous amount of research was done and data collected. Second, it was a time of unparalleled cooperation between all the interested state and federal agencies. Most of the work that year was done in the Whitefish Mountain Range on 350,000 acres within the Flathead and Kootenai National Forests.

Even the annual report, published the following March, caused few ripples. It contained a comprehensive accounting of the work done, along with an impressive amount of data. The report, however, was quick to point out it was too early in the project to begin making sweeping recommendations. But tucked within the feel-good spirit of the report were a few disconcerting mentions of recent trends. The report noted the increasing development of subdivisions in habitat frequented by grizzlies and mentioned that a large portion of grizzly territory was subject to disturbances from oil and gas exploration, as well as commercial logging. The report discussed the adverse effect potential logging could have on grizzly habitat, with the determination that an in-depth study would be done on the effects of logging on grizzly habitat and activity.

Subsequent annual reports added a tremendous amount of information to the Border Grizzly Area database, and while Jonkel was careful to avoid drawing premature conclusions, the research already pointed toward a situation that was going to create an adversarial relationship between the scientists and the national forest land managers.

A review of those national forests within the Border Grizzly Area explains why. In the late 1970s logging was king in the national forests. Though resource utilization was but one of several areas that land managers were required to oversee, there was little doubt that logging took precedence over all other activities.

I was right in the middle of all this. During the first years of the Border Grizzly Project, I held the position of design engineer on the Fisher River Ranger District in the Kootenai National Forest. This huge national forest lies to the west of the Flathead National Forest, the heart of the study area. Virtually all of the Kootenai National Forest is grizzly habitat. And we were logging it to death.

During this period each national forest was given an allowable harvest quota, which was then apportioned to each ranger district within the forest. The greater the harvest quota, the higher the budget. At the Fisher River Ranger District, we literally functioned as a logging company. Foresters feverishly sought out the best stands of mature timber to achieve the annual harvest (cut) quota, and engineers were right behind them with road-building plans. Little thought was given to the wilderness potential of the land. Once pristine mountain ranges were denuded of timber by massive clearcuts, and logging access roads contributed loads of silt and debris to streams.

My job was to oversee the survey and design of the roads accessing timber harvest areas. I admit that, at that time, I was not greatly appreciative of my responsibility to preserve grizzly bear habitat. In fact, like most forest service employees, I knew little about it. Thanks to my efforts, many miles of roads were built into pristine areas where grizzlies roamed. Loggers cut the trees and sent them to the local mill, and our harvest quotas were met.

After a while I began hearing complaints from engineering and timber harvest supervisors. Something about the mess over in the Flathead. That mess, I learned, was caused by a man named Chuck Jonkel and his Border Grizzly Project.

One day, while our timber sale administration group met in a conference room at the Fisher River Ranger Station, the chief forester held up a Border Grizzly Project report and said, "These people are looking for anything to stop logging." He threw the report onto the table, placed his hands on his hips, and said, "This thing will never fly, but if it does, it could literally put us out of work." I didn't realize it at the time, but those words would prove prophetic for me. I would not only lose my job, but also my career with the U.S. Forest Service.

Nothing happened at first. But the next year, my supervisor informed me that I would have the privilege of creating one of the first Environmental Impact Statements (EIS). This EIS was for the Bristow Timber Sale. Bristow Creek was located between Lake Kookanusa and the Yaak River country, all of which was grizzly habitat. I attacked this assignment with great zeal, explaining in detail how the logging and road building in Bristow Creek would have absolutely no adverse impact on wildlife habitat, soil or water pollution, recreation, or any other aspect of the environment. My report drew praise, even raves, from my supervisors. For a season I basked in the glow of unprecedented favor within the hierarchy of the forest service. Unfortunately, my exalted status would be short-lived.

Actually, I didn't create the problem. It was handed to me in the form of a 2-inch-thick document titled, "Federal Highway Construction Specifications." With it came an official notice that all federal road construction would henceforth conform to federal highway standards. In other words, a 12-foot-wide logging access road would now be built to the same exacting standards of a six-lane freeway.

Construction costs skyrocketed as we were forced to lay gravel on even the most obscure roads that snaked into untrammeled wilderness for miles and were utilized for just a brief period during timber harvest. As a result almost all of our timber sales ran a deficit, meaning the cost of road construction surpassed the value of the harvested timber. We were literally giving the timber away, and in some cases, even paying to have it logged. This period of madness within the Forest Service resulted in billions of dollars of lost revenue to the taxpayer.

And then I decided to do something about it. First, I complained to my supervisor that the specifications and road design packages were far too complicated and costly. He shrugged off my diatribe, so I decided to send a letter to the regional engineer in Missoula, Montana. This was before the advent of the computer or word processor, so I sent a rough draft to be typed. The next day I was called into the assistant ranger's office. He informed me that my letter had been turned in to him by a loyal girl in the typing pool, and that I should refrain from sending any more letters without his permission.

I left the office angry and frustrated. That evening, I typed up my own letter and mailed it the next morning. A week letter I was summoned to the office of the supervisor of the Kootenai National Forest. Flipping the letter at me, he said I was not a team player, and that I would never receive another pay increase or promotion as long as he was supervisor; if I decided to transfer elsewhere, he said, he would make that forest aware of my rebellious nature. "You'd best look for another line of work," he commented. "Government work isn't for you. You're just not a team player."

I walked out of that office, gathered my belongings, and quit.

Chuck Jonkel wasn't faring so well, either. The Border Grizzly Project's five-year summary report concluded that a combination of rapid habitat loss of wilderness areas due to land management pressures, increased long-range timber harvest pressures, increased gas and oil exploration, human intrusion, and a half-century of fire suppression (to save trees from burning so they could be logged) had pushed the grizzly to a threshold from which it might not be able to recover. In other words, national forest land managers were not in compliance with the Endangered Species Act.

One of the most startling findings of the study came from the analysis of the Trapper/Bigelow Timber Sale, just south of Glacier National Park in the Flathead National Forest. This area was part of the home range of three radio-collared grizzly bears. Careful monitoring of these bears during logging activity showed that all three avoided not only the active logging sites, but also the entire area encompassed by the logging access roads, even though it offered prime habitat. Other studies indicated that grizzlies generally avoided even older logged areas, and they particularly avoided areas containing logging roads, especially if there was human activity.

Consequently, the Border Grizzly Project recommended:

- No clearcuts larger than twenty acres
- No logging in moist sites (favorite feeding areas of grizzlies)
- No soil disturbance at logging sites (inhibits growth of native grizzly foods)
- No logging near snow chutes (favorite feeding areas for grizzlies)

- No logging that would destroy or damage grizzly food sources

- No logging with heavy machinery that might compact the soil and inhibit plant growth

- No logging that might damage or remove grizzly security cover

- No logging on ridge tops, creek bottoms or heads of drainages (favorite grizzly travel and feeding areas)

- No ungated logging roads (to eliminate excess human activity)

The Five-Year Border Grizzly Project Summary Report contained much valuable scientific information about the grizzly in the Northern Rockies. Unfortunately, most of it was overshadowed by the explosion of protest from the U.S. Forest Service. Overnight, land managers were brought face-to-face with the realization they could no longer clearcut entire drainages and build roads anywhere they wanted.

"All the national forests raised hell," Jonkel told me. "The Lolo, the Flathead, the Kootenai, they all put a lot of pressure on the financial end to stop the research, and that's exactly what they did. Just five years into the Border Grizzly Project, they killed it. The said they had enough data."

But if the bureaucrats thought the Border Grizzly Project would go away, they were mistaken. Environmental organizations obtained a copy of the report and filed suit in federal court against the U.S. Forest Service to bring that agency into compliance with the Endangered Species Act. The federal courts agreed. No longer could national forest employees produce whitewashed Environmental Impact Statements. The result was a drastic reduction in logging throughout grizzly country, and a moratorium on road building.

The impacts of the Border Grizzly Project's findings stretched far beyond the study area. Many of the current forest management rules practiced by the U.S. Forest Service throughout the West grew from this study, such as a maximum of twenty acres for a clearcut, mandatory setbacks of all logging and road-building activity near streams, and gates on roads to lessen human impact on wildlife.

I also received some good news two months after I quit the agency. The chief engineer of the Kootenai National Forest called and informed me that the regional engineer had indeed read my letter and agreed with me. New specifications were being examined to simplify forest road construction, which should result in more cost-efficient and environmentally compatible routes.

So, like Jonkel, I received some form of belated retribution. And like Chuck, I also received the martyr's reward. We were both jobless.

Actually, Jonkel continued doing grizzly bear research in association with the University of Montana. One of those projects was the continuation of a study begun during the Border Grizzly Project to find some method of adverse conditioning of grizzly bears. Far too many problem bears, such as aggressive and garbage-addicted animals, were being eliminated. And with the sharp increase in hikers invading grizzly country, grizzly/human incidents had also increased, and some form of bear deterrent was needed to keep both parties safe. Researchers Carrie Hunt (see chapter 8) and Martin Smith undertook the ground-breaking work of examining and testing various methods and compounds that might work as grizzly-bear deterrents.

Testing was done in two phases. The first involved laboratory tests on captive grizzly and black-bears to test their responses to various deterrents under "charging bear" conditions. The other phase would be field tests of free-ranging black bears at a garbage dump located in Sparwood, British Columbia.

The four "test" bears, one black and three grizzlies, were acquired from state and federal agencies. All of them were problem animals, habitual offenders destined to be destroyed. They were housed in an old World War II prisoner-of-war compound at Fort Missoula in Missoula, Montana.

A variety of substances, potions, noise, and combinations was used on the bears, including dog and shark repellents. The actual testing was quite interesting, especially for the tester, who entered the compound where the bear was housed and provoked the animal to charge. The most promising results came from dog repellent sprays, which caused most of the bears to retreat after being doused. Others had limited repellent value.

At one point, an umbrella-like contraption was tested, with the hope that the sudden opening would cause the startled bear to retreat, but the animals merely stood their ground. Loud noise didn't work either. In fact, it had quite the opposite effect: The animals actually became more aggressive in response to the piercing shrieks. Even loud rock 'n' roll music was tried, but the bears ignored it!

Chuck Jonkel recalled:

> The skunk urine was the worst. One day this guy showed up at my office with a bottle, claiming he had this surefire bear repellent. He proceeded to open it up in my office, and we had to vacate the place for the rest of the day. Then when we tried it on the bears and it didn't work, the guy called me and he was real upset because the skunk piss "had" to repel a bear. We wasted a lot of time and energy on stuff that didn't work, but I had a gut feeling that there was something out there that would stop an aggressive bear. We just had to find it.

Bill Pounds was another man who fervently desired something that would make him feel safe in bear country. He'd recently fulfilled his lifelong dream of moving to Montana to experience the beauty of nature, but one night a grizzly had visited his campsite and terrified Bill and his wife and young child.

> I started carrying a sawed-off shotgun for protection whenever I went into the woods, but my wife didn't feel comfortable having it around, especially with a toddler. I'd always been an entrepreneur, so when I learned that Chuck Jonkel was doing bear repellent tests at Fort Missoula, I made up some concoctions that I thought might work and took them over. None of it worked. The more stuff I sent in that failed, the more I became obsessed with finding something that would work.

DR. CHUCK JONKEL

Pounds became so frustrated that his wife talked him into taking a short vacation to Mexico. At a cantina in a sleepy little town, Pounds was visiting with the locals at the bar when one of the men presented him with a glass of cold beer and an innocuous looking red pepper.

"Take and eat," the man said, with a knowing wink at his cronies. "This is our way of honoring you."

"I knew something was up from the way they were smirking," Pounds recalled with a laugh. "So I just nibbled at the end of the pepper. Wow! My mouth was instantly on fire and I gulped the beer down. It helped, but my mouth still felt like it'd been reamed out with a hot poker. All the while the local guys were slapping my back and laughing, my mind was back in Missoula. I grabbed the guy by the arm and asked, 'What was that stuff?' The guy just shrugged and said, 'Is just red pepper, *señor.*'"

Back in Missoula, Pounds furnished ground-up red pepper to the lab, and it showed great promise. The first tests were conducted on problem bears. The animals were tethered by a 12-foot-long leg snare fastened to a tree. During the first test of the red pepper, Carrie Hunt approached the bear and it charged—but when sprayed in the face, the animal immediately retreated, rapidly blinking its eyes and pawing at its face. Succeeding tests brought the same results. In fact, bears that had been previously sprayed with red pepper took a submissive position, standing sideways to the tester, with head down and eyes averted. When the tester continued forward, the panicked animals usually ran to the end of the foot snare cable or tried climbing the tree. Now the researchers faced the problem of delivering the red pepper in a propellant that could be manufactured commercially. Eventually, Pounds succeeded in rendering the oil of capsaicin from the red pepper. This is the oily active ingredient that gives red (cayenne) pepper its hotness.

"The bear-spray tests were astounding," Jonkel recalled. "The stuff was easy to use and virtually odorless, and it caused an immediate adverse reaction from the bears. We tested it on sixty black and grizzly bears and it never failed to make a bear stop what it was doing. There's been nothing that's come close to it since."

In 1986 Bill Pounds' new company, Counter Assault, began marketing the first effective bear-deterrent spray. Unfortunately, so did others who tried to cash in on Pounds' creation. The result was poorly manufactured products that claimed to deter a bear attack but often malfunctioned, *resulting* in several bear attacks. The Environmental Protection Agency became involved and set minimum standards for the potency of the red pepper capsaicin, and for the propellant that delivered the red pepper. Only EPA-registered products can be sold as "bear spray." Today's EPA-approved bear spray delivers an airborne red pepper in an orange fog that reaches out 30 feet in distance and 10 feet wide in milliseconds.

While some outdoor recreationists have remained skeptical about using anything that comes in a can to stop a bear attack, the facts are irrefutable. Stephen Herrero, a leading bear expert, petitioned various state, federal, and private groups whose employees spent much of their time in bear country. His study determined that almost 90 percent of those people who used bear spray succeeded in stopping or lessening the severity of a bear attack. Alaska wildlife biologist Tom Smith has even created a database on bear attacks and told me that people attacked by bears successfully thwarted the charge 90 percent of the time when using bear spray; those who used a firearm, on the other hand, were successful only 50 percent of the time.

My own investigation garnered similar results. I wrote a book called *True Stories of Bear Attacks: Who Survived and Why,* which related the successful use of bear spray to thwart thirty bear attacks. I also interviewed three people who were unable to stop an attack even though they used bear spray. However, two of those people admitted they had used, cheap, non–EPA-registered sprays.

In the single instance when an EPA-registered bear spray did not stop an attacking grizzly, extenuating circumstances may have contributed to the apparent failure of the bear spray. Matt Pelland and his wife, Tracy, were on a day hike up the Cracker Lake Trail on the east side of Glacier National Park on a brisk October morning in 1998 when they surprised a sow grizzly with cubs 40 yards away on a brushy bend in the trail. The sow charged, and Tracy instinctively turned and ran—a behavior that experts say is likely to trigger a predatory response in a grizzly. The bear knocked Tracy to the ground, and bit and shook her. Matt, still fumbling to get the bear spray out of its hip holster, ran up to the bear yelling and waving his arms. The animal swung its head around, spotted Matt and leveled him with a single blow. As the bear bit at Matt's leg, he remembers spraying the animal in the face without apparent effect.

Tracy lay on the ground in shock, but was urged on by Matt's yelling, "Run, Tracy! Run!"

She lurched to her feet and stumbled down the trail, at which point the sow left Matt and pounced on the woman again. When Matt looked up, he saw the bear standing over his fallen wife, but not savaging her. To engage the bear again, Matt felt, would only invite a fresh wave of attacks. His wife would need help, so he plunged into the creek bottom and ran for help.

In the meantime, Tracy, curled into a tight ball, awaited the inevitable mauling, but the bear merely stood over her, wheezing and coughing. And then the bear did the unthinkable. It laid down on top of her. "That was the worst part of the attack. That, and not knowing what condition Matt was in," Tracy told me during a phone interview. "The bear was so heavy she almost suffocated me, and I got bear spray from the bear's fur in my eyes."

Eventually the grizzly walked off, and Tracy hurried down the trail. A half hour later she met a relieved Matt and a team of park service rangers. After an emotional reunion, Tracy and Matt were taken to a hospital, treated for their injuries, and released the next day.

To fully assess this incident, I sought the opinion of a respected bear biologist, Barrie Gilbert, who had also been attacked by a sow grizzly while doing research in Yellowstone National Park. More than a thousand stitches were required to patch his torn body. "Let's put this entire incident in proper perspective," Gilbert began. "The bear knocked down both the man and woman, and it had its way with the woman twice. And they only spend one day in the hospital? It sounds to me like the bear spray worked! People have got to remember that bear spray is a deterrent. It's not security in a can. It's supposed to stop or deter a bear attack, and in this case that's exactly what it did."

The value of bear spray to protect humans is a proven fact. And bear spray has also saved hundreds of grizzly bears that otherwise would have been shot either during or after an attack. And since most attacks involve a hiker surprising a protective sow grizzly with cubs, the impact on the bear population becomes even greater.

One of the most vivid examples of bear spray saving a sow grizzly with cubs from certain death occurred on an early June morning in 1998, when Cody, Wyoming, resident Jeff Buckingham and his pal, Cory Nuss, set off to gather elk antlers in the North Fork of the Shoshone River. About 30 miles northwest of Cody, some 20,000 elk winter on the open side hills of this country during the winter months. The bulls shed their antlers, which may weigh as much as thirty pounds, and fetch anywhere from $7 to $10 per pound from craftsmen, who turn the antlers into everything from buttons and knife handles to chandeliers. Both young men were sophomores at the University of Wyoming and relied on their earnings from antler picking to finance a large part of their college tuition.

After three days of sleeping under trees and subsisting on a meager diet of Ramen noodles, both men had gathered about one hundred pounds of antlers. It was time to return to their pickup parked 4 miles away at a trailhead. The departure couldn't come soon enough for Cory Nuss—he was worried about bears. They'd seen quite a bit of grizzly sign, tracks and scat, and quite frankly he was spooked. Jeff Buckingham had appeased his friend by bringing along a .44 magnum pistol and a can of bear spray, which he gave to Cory.

Burdened by the weight of the antlers and weary from their trip, the men trudged down the main trail, following along a creek. With every step closer to the pickup, their vigilance subsided. As they approached a grove of dense timber, Cory was in the lead when he glanced up and spotted two grizzly cubs 50 yards away. He skidded to a halt and, gesturing wildly, alerted Jeff. Both men stood silently, hoping the cubs would wander off, but one of them ambled in their direction, spotted the men, and squealed in terror.

A moment later a large dark-brown sow grizzly burst out of the timber and stood on her hind legs, swiveling her head back and forth and sniffing. The bear's eyes locked onto Cory, and she immediately charged. The sow picked up speed and came at them low to the ground, teeth bared, ears back. Jeff pulled his pistol and aimed between the bear's eyes, while Cory extended his arm, bear spray in hand, and flipped off the safety tab.

Jeff recalled, "I cocked the pistol and was squeezing the trigger when Cory sent a blast of bear spray into the bear's face. The sow stopped about 15 feet away, staggered backwards, coughing and gagging and swiping at her face. Then she whirled and raced back to her cubs and disappeared into the forest." Jeff added with great emphasis, "I was *that* close to killing that sow."

The contributions that Chuck Jonkel has made to the conservation of the grizzly are immense. His directorship of the Border Grizzly Project not only exposed the problems and excesses of state, federal, and private land managers in grizzly country, but also laid the groundwork for proper stewardship by private industry of all wildlands where the grizzly and other sensitive wildlife roam.

These accomplishments alone would be enough, but Chuck Jonkel's resolute drive to assist in discovering a bear deterrent that would keep both man and bear safe rates as one of the greatest accomplishments in the history of grizzly-bear conservation.

And at seventy-six years of age, Chuck has no plans of slowing down. In spring and summer he routinely leads grizzly-bear field trips for such prestigious conservation organizations as the Nature Conservancy and the Glacier Institute. Every fall, Chuck leads an expedition to Churchill, Manitoba, to teach polar-bear biology to bear enthusiasts.

He's also been vocal in condemning what he calls the "Hollywood Syndrome," a recent trend in nature films toward titillating and inaccurate depictions of the grizzly bear. Chuck warns that this trend has spawned a host of supposed bear whisperers—attention-grabbing men like Timothy Treadwell, who claimed to possess special powers to communicate with grizzlies. Treadwell appeared on numerous television talk shows—such as David Letterman, Tom Snyder, Rosie O'Donnell—and on nature channels such as Animal Planet and Discovery, claiming grizzly bears are misunderstood and that man and beast can become friends. But on October 5, 2003, Treadwell and his friend, Amie Huguenard, were killed and eaten by brown grizzly bears in Alaska. In response, investigators killed the two bears.

As the director of the Great Bear Foundation, Chuck mentors a core of young men and women seeking guidance, purpose, and professional procedure to match their enthusiasm for saving the great bear and its habitat. Carrie Hunt, who also helped develop bear spray, spoke of Chuck with gratitude.

> I owe so much to that man. He took me under his wing when I was an undergraduate student with no qualifications. He gave me a chance to accomplish bear research projects in a world that was off-limits to women. He's produced a solid core of men and women like myself who are willing to take up the standard for bear conservation.

Carrie added with a laugh, "I guess you could say we're the next generation of grizzled old men—and women!"

TODAY'S STANDARD BEARERS
THE NEW BREED OF GRIZZLED OLD MEN AND WOMEN

As inspiring as it is to read about the courage and tenacity of the grizzled old men featured in the previous chapters, there is also a sense of loss and discouragement. Some of these extraordinary patriarchs who stood in the gap to staunch the flow of grizzly-bear blood have passed on, and others await their final sunset.

The good news is that the cupboard is not bare. Far from it, in fact, for a new breed of men and women have arisen to take up the cause of grizzly conservation. Most have been either directly mentored by these grizzled old men or indirectly by their writings and actions. Thanks to the groundwork laid by their predecessors, today's conservationists are fortunate to work for federal, state, or private agencies, which furnish a comfortable salary.

One of the most prominent is Chris Servheen, grizzly bear coordinator of the U.S. Fish & Wildlife Service, who was mentored by Chuck Jonkel while he was a graduate student at the University of Montana during the historic Border Grizzly Study. Servheen now holds sway over all grizzly-bear programs on federal lands.

Then there is Tom Smith, research wildlife biologist for the U.S. Geological Survey Alaska Science Center, who has become one of the most outspoken proponents of the use of bear spray. Tom's carefully crafted press releases sometimes cause a stir within the bear community, such as the study he released that exposed the dangers of the incorrect use of bear spray as a bear repellent. (Smith had noticed that people in bear country had begun spraying pepper spray around or on their boats and equipment in the mistaken belief that the red pepper would repel a bear. The opposite was true, for inert red pepper is an attractant to a curious bear.) In addition, Smith has compiled an exhaustive computer database of bear attacks, which proves that bear spray has stopped 90 percent of bear charges, while firearms have stopped onrushing bears only about half the time.

Dogs following the scent of a bear around a barn

WIND RIVER BEAR INSTITUTE

On the state level we find Montana bear specialist Jamie Jonkel carrying on his father's legacy with the same dedication and tenacity. Stephen Stringham, a professor at the University of Alaska in Soldatna, has produced studies on bear body language that have been instrumental in teaching the public how to monitor a bear's emotional state by the way the animal postures its body.

In the private sector are Louisa Wilcox, director for the privately funded Natural Resources Defense Council, who works tirelessly to preserve grizzly habitat, and Joyce Oats of the Glacier Institute, who directs grizzly-bear field trips and seminars for visitors to Glacier National Park.

The list of people who have taken up the standard for the great bear is too long to note here, especially without running a risk of overlooking people who labor in obscurity. However, Carrie Hunt, Chuck Bartlebaugh, and Doug Peacock are three private-sector bear conservationists who particularly impress me. All three have dedicated their lives to saving the great bear, without a salary and with tenuous or nonexistent funding. The following chapters illuminate their lives and remind us that even today a few unselfish, committed people can have a tremendous impact on the grizzly's welfare.

CHAPTER 8

⊷•⊶ ⊷•⊶ ⊷•⊶

CARRIE HUNT

USING BEAR DOGS AND TOUGH LOVE TO SAVE PROBLEM BEARS

Imprisoned within a steel culvert trap, the three-year-old male grizzly paws at the welded gate. Yesterday evening this teenage bear sneaked into the horse barn of a rural home near the Crowsnest Pass area of Southwest Alberta to steal grain. Today he was instead lured into the culvert trap by the tantalizing odor of rancid road-killed deer.

Now, two hours after dawn, the young bear is frantic to escape. People are yelling and banging on the trap with iron rods. But worst of all, two devilish dogs are barking furiously at the rear gate.

Suddenly, the entrance gate is raised and the grizzly scrambles out, only to be met by explosions and a fusillade of rubber bullets and bean bags painfully pounding its rump. The bear bawls in fear and outrage and gallops for the safety of the dense forest 80 yards away, but before the bear gets there, the dogs are after him, barking furiously. The frantic bear dives into the forest, and the dogs suddenly break off and retreat. At last the terrified animal feels safe, far from the horse barn, and the banging and blasting and barking.

Though the above incident may look and sound chaotic, the entire episode was carefully planned in advance, choreographed by bear biologist Carrie Hunt. It's called aversive conditioning, a revolutionary concept Hunt invented to teach grizzly bears to associate humans and their habitations with intense discomfort. "That's how aversive conditioning works," Hunt told me when I visited her at the Wind River Bear Institute compound near Florence, Montana.

> Grizzly bears are quick learners. It doesn't take a bear long to figure out where to find easy human food at a rural home site, and we apply the aversive conditioning to teach it to associate human habitations with an unpleasant experience. Then we set an imaginary boundary the bear cannot cross. In this case, it was the dense forest behind the horse barn. When the Karelian bear dogs got to the forest, the dogs' handlers called them off, which set in the bear's mind that anything in the thicket is safe, but anything closer is a place of terror and pain.
>
> Nobody thought such a thing as bear shepherding, as we call it, was possible, but it has been done, and without serious injury to bears, or people or the dogs. Our results are real head-turners. In just the last three years, the state of Montana credits us with saving the lives of eighteen grizzlies.

Saving eighteen endangered grizzlies is an astounding achievement, but for Carrie Hunt, it's just another accomplishment in a stellar career dedicated to saving the great bear. To say that Hunt's career in bear management began early is an understatement. "I was only eight years old when I decided to study and work with large predators," Hunt informed me. "My mother had given me Rudyard Kipling's *Jungle Book*. I was mesmerized by his stories of large predators. I think I wore the book out. All the large predators interested me, but since the grizzly was the largest predator in the West, I decided that I would become a wildlife biologist and study grizzlies."

Hunt faced one small problem: There weren't many grizzlies living in Berkeley, California, where she was born. Her father, an exploration geologist for Anaconda Copper Company, took a job in the ore-rich Andes Mountains in South America. Hunt spent her childhood years hiking the mountain trails, exulting in the high country. It was missing only one thing—bears. "I know it sounds crazy, but even back then, I knew I'd study grizzlies, and I'd use dogs to study them. I always had dogs around me, and I saw the way a loyal dog would protect me and respond to my commands. I realize it was just a little girl's musings, but I really did believe even back then that dogs could somehow be used to manage grizzlies."

When it came time for Hunt to choose a college, it was a no-brainer. "It was the University of Montana," She said with an emphatic nod. "Montana was the only state that had a grizzly population in the 1980s, and I knew Chuck Jonkel was a professor of biology there."

Upon graduation, possessing an impressive portfolio of bear research papers, Hunt readily found work in the world of bear management, but not the kind she was particularly interested in.

> A lot of the projects I worked on were interesting and they did some good, but there was also a lot of bureaucratic wrangling that I didn't like. I wanted to get out in the field and do something great for the grizzly.
>
> I was also kind of frustrated. Here we had the grizzly on the Endangered Species List, yet we were still killing them off. And the most offensive thing about all of it was that bear managers were doing all the killing. Sure, it was problem bears they were killing, but I just couldn't accept their definition of a "problem" bear, which amounted to some poor bear that got caught eating food scraps from a garbage can behind someone's house. I couldn't get it out of my head because I had been around grizzlies enough to know that they are quick learners. If they could learn bad habits so quickly, they could be taught just as quickly to avoid areas where they were getting into trouble.

The idea of using Karelian bear dogs was an evolutionary thing, according to Hunt. Back in the early 1980s, when she was testing bear deterrents on laboratory animals, she noticed how the bears quickly learned and reacted to her body language when she approached them with pepper spray. After experiencing the effects of a snoot full of red pepper, a bear would act submissive the next time Hunt entered their enclosure and would run away as soon as she extended her hand—whether or not she held a can of pepper spray.

"That's when I first got the notion," Hunt said, "that if I could communicate with bears with simple hand movements, then maybe I could figure out some way to communicate to them where I didn't want them to be."

Hunt's first chance to work a grizzly occurred in 1986 while she was the assistant director of Wyoming's grizzly bear program. "We really didn't have any idea what to do with the grizzlies that were migrating south of Yellowstone National Park," Hunt said.

> The North Fork Shoshone River Road, which was the main road south of the park, had a history of grizzly problems. The bears would show up alongside the road, and tourists would feed them or press in close for photos.
>
> I got the idea to try aversive conditioning on bear 104, a sow grizzly with two cubs that was hanging close to the road every day. She was absolutely oblivious to the people. I drove up one day, and bear 104 was feeding on a winter-killed elk carcass; and there must have been twenty people within 100 feet of her taking pictures. I don't know what kept her from charging and hurting one of those people.
>
> I decided it was time to get her away from the road. One day I found her feeding on dandelions along the edge of the road. I shot her three times with rubber bullets, and she bellowed and howled and bit at her rump before galloping into the forest. I worked bear 104 for a month that year, and the next spring I worked her a week. After that she stayed away from the road and trouble.
>
> Officials were ready to kill bear 104 when I first began working with her. But thanks to the aversive conditioning program, she lived for fifteen years after that and produced four litters of cubs. After my success with

Carrie Hunt and Jewel

WIND RIVER BEAR INSTITUTE

bear 104, I was hooked on the concept of aversive conditioning because I saw for myself how quickly I could make a grizzly understand what I wanted it to do.

Even with such a promising start, Hunt was not totally satisfied with the results. The biggest problem was that the bears, being quick learners, began putting some distance between themselves and the people using rubber bullets and pepper spray. "That's really when I started seriously thinking about using dogs," she said. "We needed something to reach out a little farther than 25 yards (the effective range of a rubber bullet), and I knew bears hated dogs yapping at them."

Hunt began suggesting to bear biologists the use of dogs as part of the aversive conditioning program, but initially officials weren't interested. Then she remembered a conversation she'd had with Norwegian bear biologist Ivar Mysterud, who used Karelian bear dogs to sniff out bear sign in his home country. A U.S. Forest Service biologist who had heard one of Hunt's lectures on adverse conditioning and the potential role for dogs phoned Carrie in 1990. He told her he had purchased a pair of Karelian bear dogs and the female had recently produced a litter of pups. Hunt was invited to come over and pick one out for herself.

"I walked into the room where the pups were playing, and immediately my eyes met the sweetest little female that I called Cassie. We hit it off, and after I'd trained her, we worked black bears in New Mexico," Hunt said. "Cassie was absolutely amazing. She sniffed out bears, chased them out of yards and taught me a lot about where the bears had been and why they were there."

A second Karelian, a male, was added in 1994, and besides working together with startling efficiency, the pair produced a litter of pups.

Hunt's first opportunity to use a team of bear dogs came in Yosemite National Park, where black bears were notorious for invading campgrounds and helping themselves to food, sometimes literally peeling the top off a vehicle to get at the food stored inside. "These were the most incorrigible bears in the world," Hunt told me, "but the Karelians and the aversive conditioning program with the Karelians was a big success."

Hunt eventually founded the Wind River Bear Institute (WRBI) and developed the program called bear shepherding. Essentially, bear shepherding reduces conflicts between humans and bears and subsequently reduced human-caused mortalities among bears, which account for the vast majority of bear deaths. Traditional management techniques have been limited to removal and relocation of problem bears, which only takes the focus off cleaning up the attractants that created the problem in the first place. With relocation the problem doesn't really go away. It just moves to wherever the problem bear ends up, which then results in a public relations problem when people learn that a particular bear released in their area was a troublemaker elsewhere. A whopping 80 percent of relocated bears are eventually killed because this method treats the symptoms but doesn't eliminate the root causes of the problem bear's behavior.

To date, bear shepherding is the only successful solution to this problem. However, the WRBI goes a step beyond simply educating bears; it also educates people. Hunt's program, called "Partners-In-Life," has the goal of educating not only the bears but also the public residing in bear country. Human prevention work is done by going on-site with landowners who are experiencing bear problems. Hunt explained:

> Probably 75 percent of our time afield is spent going door-to-door educating residents about proper food and garbage storage. We go in and teach people to be more careful with food offerings around their place that a bear might find attractive. A lot of the attractants are easy to eliminate. Like pet food. We suggest feeding the dog and cat indoors to keep bears from pet food. Bird feeders should be placed 20 feet above the ground out of reach of bears, or put out during winter months while the bears are hibernating. Besides, that's when the birds need the feed the most.
>
> Garbage is the number one bear attractant. We teach people to secure their garbage in bear-proof containers, and to make sure the garbage is enclosed in double garbage bags that are tightly sealed to lessen odor. Really, a bear doesn't have much reason to approach a home site unless there's a food reward offered. Take away the food, and the bear problem largely disappears.

The Karelian bear dogs are at the heart of the WRBI's bear-shepherding program. These black-and-white dogs weigh only about fifty pounds, but they affect a bear slated for aversive conditioning much more than yelling humans and rubber bullets. The dogs' aggressive, fearless nature and threatening bark is the primary component of the bear's aversive conditioning. The dogs set the boundaries for the bear when they break off contact, and also act as a safety buffer between their handlers and any bear that might turn back to confront the management team. Karelians also possess excellent trailing instincts and are often used to track down problem bears for aversive conditioning in the field. Hunt gushed, as she stroked one of three dogs vying for her affection in a two-acre enclosure, one of four at the WRBI kennels.

> They're my babies, but they really don't make good house pets. We get far too many calls from people who read about the Karelian bear dogs and then go out and buy one, only to find out that the breed is very independent and aloof. They just have so much energy that you have to either keep them kenneled or tied up. Otherwise, they're off to do what they were bred for—hunting. Even then, we've found that only about one dog out of a litter will have the courage to stand up to a bear. It takes close to 1,000 hours to teach that one special dog to obey the handler's voice commands—to stay, come, bark.

Of the hundreds of bears administered aversive conditioning by the WRBI, only a bear named Stahr had to be removed from the wild. The sordid details surrounding this single failure still rankle Hunt. Stahr's story began in 1997, when residents of Polebridge, a tiny village on the banks of the North Fork Flathead River along the western edge of Glacier National Park, began to notice an increase in bear activity. Grizzly sightings normally averaged one or two bears annually, but beginning that summer, more than a dozen grizzlies were seen roaming the area. And they were acting strangely. In the past wandering bears ran away when confronted by humans, but now the animals walked brazenly through front yards. Tim Manley, bear management specialist for the state of Montana, was contacted, but he was at a loss to explain the sudden increase in bear activity.

That fall a U.S. Forest Service survey crew phoned Manley and complained about a large number of grizzlies in the area where they were working along the edge of town. When Tim investigated, he was shocked to find fifty-pound sacks of corn, oats, and barley strewn on the ground around the property of a man who was a wildlife photographer.

"There was bear scat filled with grain all over the place," Manley told me. "The feed was so thick on the ground that it would require machinery to get it all up."

When confronted, the photographer claimed it was simply left-over grain from winter feeding of deer and elk, but he promised to stop putting it out. State wildlife officials were so concerned with the remaining grain that they strung an electric fence around the property to keep bears out.

Manley and Hunt worked long hours for several weeks, using aversive conditioning to put the fear of humans back into the bears and to set boundaries they would not cross. One of the bears they became particularly interested in was a young grizzly they named Stahr, a sow that had two cubs. Female grizzlies like Stahr were considered critical to maintaining a viable population in the North Fork area because she could be counted upon to produce two cubs every other year for a decade or more.

The next winter the property owner announced his intentions to again feed deer and elk in the winter. Manley paid another visit and strongly advised against it. The man compromised and said he would place the grain on his frozen pond. That way, he explained, by the time the bears came out of hibernation in the spring, the grain would have sunk to the bottom. "I just shook my head at the guy's reasoning," Manley commented, "but at the time there was no law against it."

The next spring, Manley tracked a radio-collared female grizzly to the photographer's property and a pile of bird seed hidden behind a log in the man's backyard. A quick search by Manley uncovered other piles of bird seed and grain behind logs and stumps.

When confronted, the man claimed the grain was spread around to feed ducks. "He had always maintained that the grain had not been put out to lure bears in," Manley fumed, "but from that point on, I was convinced that's exactly why he was placing the grain out."

Then fate intervened. One day while Manley awaited a connecting flight in the Salt Lake City airport, he visited a magazine shop and began idly thumbing through a respected wildlife magazine. Then he noticed an article authored by the wildlife photographer. "I almost screamed when I looked at the cover photo in the article," Tim recalled. "It was of a sow grizzly and cub climbing on a supposedly abandoned bird feeder. I knew exactly where that bird feeder was located. It was 20 feet behind the guy's back door!"

Confronted with the irrefutable proof of his wrongdoings, the man still denied that he was baiting grizzlies onto his property to photograph them. "It's ironic," Manley noted. "The guy's article was about the mistakes people make when living in bear country, yet he was doing exactly the thing he was writing against. It's sad, but once again it's the bears that pay the price. The cub shown in that photo was eventually killed with a belly full of bird seed."

Aversive conditioning was again used on the bears that had been lured back to the hidden grain. Among those bears were Stahr and her cubs. Hunt remembers giving them a good dose of aversive conditioning with her Karelian bear dogs. Afterward, residents in the area were urged to remove any unsecured food so Stahr and the other bears would not be tempted to return. The treatment seemed to work: Stahr stayed clear of human habitations for a year and a half. "We were confident that our treatment was a huge success," Hunt commented. "We thought we had her turned around. We thought we'd shown that even a bear that had been tearing down doors to get at human food could be rehabilitated."

But then the WRBI funding dried up in 2000, and Hunt was unable to monitor Stahr's activities. Unfortunately, Stahr was lured back to the Polebridge area by residents who had become lax about keeping food out of her reach. Unbeknownst to Manley and Hunt, Stahr had again begun nosing around homes. People saw her, watched her, and were sometimes even entertained by her as she fed on dog food, horse grain, and food left out for her in people's backyards. They may as well have fed her poison.

The final straw for Stahr was a midnight raid at the Home Ranch Store in Polebridge, during which Stahr and her cubs literally peeled the storefront siding away to get at the food inside. Stahr had become hopelessly habituated to human food.

"Before we live-trapped her," Hunt recalled, "we gave her a few last days of freedom, and we followed her. That was a real eye-opener. She took us around to bird feeders, horse barns, and snacks left out for her, and she took us to residents who merely shrugged and said, 'Yup, she's been coming around for quite a while.' Obviously these people had ignored our instructions on smart living in bear country." Eventually, Stahr and her cubs were live-trapped and shipped to a research facility in Washington state.

Carrie Hunt's success with her bear shepherding program has not happened by accident. She works very hard at it, spending virtually every minute of every day working dogs, chasing bears, contacting landowners, or seeking grants to keep her privately funded WRBI afloat. Carrie's goal is to create a nationwide, and then a worldwide, bear-shepherding program to manage problem bears without killing them.

And Hunt seeks no glory for herself. "A while back, National Geographic contacted me and wanted to make a movie about my life," she commented at a recent "Urban Bear Management" seminar I attended. "They wanted to use Helen Hunt to portray me. I was flattered, but I just didn't have the time to spend on a movie. It might have made me famous, but my priorities lie elsewhere. I have dogs to train, people to train, bears to save. Those are my priorities." Amen. Preach it, sister!

CHAPTER 9

◄•→ ≡≼◆≽≡ ►•→•← ≡≼◆≽≡ ►•→•← ≡≼◆≽≡ →•►

CHUCK BARTLEBAUGH

ENSURING PROPER BEHAVIOR
IN BEAR COUNTRY

Dear Chuck,

Thank you for your letter and efforts of the Center for Wildlife Information. I, too, feel strongly that the Grizzly Bear is the last great symbol of wilderness. How may I help?

Sincerely,
H. Norman Schwarzkopf
General, U.S. Army
Commander in Chief
Operation Desert Storm

Chuck Bartlebaugh's early adult life showed no indication that he would one day become a leading proponent for wildlife stewardship in bear country. Instead of pristine wilderness and fresh mountain air, Chuck's first love involved driving a McLaren 200 miles per hour on winding road courses.

He loved cars—the faster, the better. While many speed freaks got their start behind the wheel of a hot rod, burning down the back streets of their home town, Chuck's rise to prominence in the world of Indy racing began methodically. After graduating high school in Rochester, Michigan, Bartlebaugh contacted racing teams and volunteered his services. In the early 1970s, he achieved the exalted position of driver of these elite road racing machines. "For me, there was no adrenalin rush to racing," he told me during our interview. "I found it to be relaxing. Sitting behind the wheel of one of the fastest sports cars in the world with a wall of photographers taking your picture before you left the pit created a sense of euphoria."

Bartlebaugh raced in the Canadian-American Challenge Cup Series, driving an English-built McLaren designed by a team of aerospace engineers and competed against Porches, Ferraris, and Lolas. Bartlebaugh also began driving in an Indy champ car series and was being groomed for the Indianapolis 500. When the oil embargo in the late 1970s put corporate-sponsored programs on hold, Bartlebaugh's racing sponsorships evaporated, ending his hopes for a racing career.

He then started his own marketing agency specializing in marketing trends and events in shopping malls.

I was conducting a market study for the recreation industry, asking people what they would like to do in the outdoors, and a surprising number of them said they'd like to go to Yellowstone National Park and feed the bears. I found this to be very troubling. Then one night I sat riveted to the television set and watched John and Frank Craighead on the *Today Show* explaining how much trouble the grizzlies in Yellowstone were in.

I decided to get involved with saving the grizzly. I went out and purchased the very best camera equipment including an 800-millimeter telephoto lens. My idea was to show the grizzly in its natural habitat and carry the Craigheads' conservation message to the public with my photography.

Bartlebaugh arrived at Cooke City, Yellowstone's northeast entrance, dressed in the latest Eddie Bauer khaki photographer's outfit, including a multipocketed vest bulging with film. He stopped at a bar for a drink and the bartender asked what had brought him to Cooke City. Bartlebaugh replied, "I'm here to photograph grizzlies."

CHUCK BARTLEBAUGH

The bartender eyed him with disdain. "The last thing we need around here is another asshole with a camera getting killed, and our bears shot up," he snapped. The remark led to a long evening of banter, which culminated with Chuck Bartlebaugh being introduced to a local forest service ranger, who took the former race-car driver under his wing.

The first thing the ranger had Bartlebaugh do was change out of the designer khaki pants and into blue jeans. Then he took Bartlebaugh into the backcountry to teach him about bears. Bartlebaugh was stunned by what he learned. It turned out that many activities carried out in the presence of bears by Bartlebaugh and other wildlife photographers were wrong! By continually moving in on the animals, photographers inadvertently stressed, harassed, and provoked them.

A few months later, Bartlebaugh and two fellow wildlife enthusiasts were having a few drinks at the Northern Lights Saloon in Polebridge, a tiny hamlet on the northwest corner of Glacier National Park. All three men were lamenting the lack of constraint most people showed around bears and wildlife in general, and the fact that there was no organization to publicize bear-avoidance safety techniques and responsible actions around wildlife. The men decided that one of them should start a grassroots organization to educate the public. But who? No one volunteered, so they decided the matter in typical barroom fashion—they drew straws. "I guess you could say I got the short end of the stick," Bartlebaugh quipped. "Frankly, I think the whole thing was a setup."

Bartlebaugh continued photographing bears, but took the then-unprecedented step of avoiding close contact. And he began to see how very wrong most people acted around them. One day, while he was photographing a sow grizzly feeding within sight of a road near the south entrance of Yellowstone National Park, a tour bus carrying senior citizens pulled up. Not content to enjoy the bear from the bus, several of these folks with cameras urged others to approach the grizzly so they could be photographed.

"I was stunned!" Bartlebaugh recalled.

These people had just passed a sign along the road informing them that it was illegal to approach grizzly bears. Some of these people had to be helped over the guardrails, and yet they were approaching within a few feet of a grizzly bear. They had no idea of the danger they were putting themselves in or the stress they were causing the bear. So I intervened and started helping them back over the guardrails back to the bus. That incident really solidified my determination to educate the public about how to enjoy wildlife, especially bears, safely and responsibly.

Shortly thereafter, Bartlebaugh created the nonprofit organization aptly called The Center for Wildlife Information (CWI). For the first few years, he enlisted volunteers to observe and interview visitors to national parks and forests. Hundreds of inappropriate actions by park visitors were documented as people from all over the United States and the world were interviewed in a nonconfrontational manner. For instance a survey in the heart of grizzly country in Yellowstone National Park found that 64 percent of all people who visited had no idea what the appropriate distance for safe bear viewing should be. The study conducted by Chuck and Eastern Michigan University students and professors was published in the *Yellowstone Science Journal.*

"What we discovered," Bartlebaugh explained, "was that people just didn't realize they were doing things that were dangerous to themselves, and to wildlife. Like walking up to bison in Yellowstone, which is one of the most dangerous things a tourist can do in the park. Or approaching a grizzly feeding alongside a road. When we interviewed people who were doing these types of things, they explained that they thought the animals were tame because they'd seen wildlife celebrities on TV approaching wild animals."

One of the most graphic examples of how a little education can sway public opinion about proper safety techniques around wild animals was a wildlife display that CWI placed in ten regional shopping malls in Michigan and Minnesota. The display was viewed by over a million shoppers and was manned by communications graduate students from various colleges, who interviewed more than 800 observers.

Phase one of the display—with photos but no verbiage explaining how to be safe around wild animals—evaluated the general public's preconceptions regarding appropriate actions around wildlife by observing their reactions and soliciting comments. People responded to the wildlife display by boasting about their own experiences getting close to, and sometimes even feeding, wildlife.

Phase two evaluated the public's reaction to the wildlife display after signs were added emphasizing wildlife stewardship and explaining proper safety techniques to use when hiking, camping, viewing, and photographing wildlife. The public responded to this display with a strong stewardship message by explaining to their children and each other the importance of acting responsibly around wildlife. Bartlebaugh explained:

> We discovered that the vast majority of people who acted inappropriately around wildlife did so because they didn't know any better. They were just acting out what they'd seen wildlife celebrities do on television nature programs. We then turned to the networks and began examining their nature-based programs, plus outdoor and nature videos. We were disturbed to learn that roughly the equivalent of $50 million dollars was being spent annually on nature-related programs and books that blatantly showed inappropriate actions by humans around wild animals and misinformation about approaching wild animals, especially bears.
>
> From our research, we developed wildlife safety education programs to make the public aware that certain actions around wild animals were inappropriate, and if they really cared about the animals, they'd also teach others how to act safely and responsibly as well.

Desert Storm war hero General Norman Schwarzkopf, who led the lightning strike that crushed the feared Republican Guard of Iraq's

*General H. Norman Schwarzkopf (left) with
Chuck Bartlebaugh (right)*

CENTER FOR WILDLIFE INFORMATION

Saddam Hussein, was so impressed with CWI's educational program that he agreed to serve as spokesman for the Be Bear Aware and Wildlife Stewardship Campaign. Nicknamed "The Bear," Schwarzkopf is a fervent supporter of grizzly-bear conservation who occasionally tours bear country to spread the message for grizzly-bear recovery and responsible wildlife stewardship. During an excursion through

Yellowstone National Park, Schwarzkopf worked hard to share his message with the public and media.

Unfortunately, not everyone got the message. A tourist who stood among a cluster of twenty people gawking at a sow grizzly and cubs, sneaked up behind the foraging bears and playfully swatted one of the cubs on the rump. The cub squealed in terror, and the sow went ballistic. She charged to within a few feet of the terrified man. The sow stood on her hind legs and roared in the intruder's face, then ran back to her cubs. The irresponsible visitor was fortunate to get off with just a warning.

When General Schwarzkopf learned of the incident, he sadly shook his head and, in an understatement that most certainly tested his years of diplomacy, called the man's actions "stupid."

While perusing the assortment of CWI brochures during my visit to Chuck's office in Missoula, Montana, I noticed one entitled, "Wildlife Viewing and Photographing Guide." This excellent publication, to my knowledge, is the only document that instructs wildlife photographers to maintain a safe distance to avoid stressing the bears and precipitating a flight-or-fight response. With sadness I recalled two incidents— one in Glacier National Park, the other in Yellowstone—during which two over-enthusiastic wildlife photographers pressured retreating grizzlies and were mauled to death.

In Yellowstone amateur photographer Bill Tesinsky followed a retreating young grizzly into a secluded draw. The bear had an orange radio collar around its neck, and Tesinsky may have been trying to get tight head shots of the bear that would not show the plastic collar. The frightened bear misread Tesinsky's actions as aggressive and turned on him. When rangers arrived on the scene after noticing Tesinsky's car illegally parked, they found the young grizzly feeding on Tesinsky's remains. Consequently, the decision was made to kill the bear.

A year later, wildlife photographer Chuck Gibbs spotted a sow grizzly with two cubs from the road that runs along the southern edge of Glacier National Park. Gibbs left his wife parked in the vehicle and hurried after the retreating sow. When he failed to return, his wife alerted authorities, who eventually discovered his ravaged body and camera equipment. When the film in the camera was developed, the initial group of photographs showed sow and cubs amiably feeding at a distance. But as the bears loomed larger in succeeding frames, the sow's demeanor changed. In the last few photos, she is standing tensely 60 yards away and staring back at Gibbs, then advancing toward him. Because rangers felt the sow was acting in self-defense and had not fed on Gibbs' body, the decision was made to spare her life.

"If those men had followed the recommendations in that brochure," Bartlebaugh commented with a frown, "they'd be alive today. The key with photographers, or for anyone traveling in bear country, is to maintain a safe and responsible distance. If people would just take a few common-sense precautions in bear country, there'd be a lot less people hurt, and a whole lot less bears killed."

Inappropriate actions by people around wild animals remain a constant source of chagrin for Bartlebaugh, who has photographed many people whose actions put themselves and the animals in danger. One time he was photographing elk in Yellowstone when he noticed a young girl moving dangerously close to a feeding bull elk. The girl's mother asked Bartlebaugh if he would take a picture of the girl smiling at the camera next to the elk.

"I can't right now, I'm too busy," he replied.

Noticing that he was trained on the elk and girl anyway, she asked, "Why not?"

"Because," Bartlebaugh shot back, "I'm too busy getting ready to get a shot of a little girl getting gored by a bull elk."

Despite CWI's relative success in educating the public, Bartlebaugh remains frustrated by television's recurring habit of showing inappropriate actions by TV celebrities around bears and other wildlife. "When people see something on television," he explained, "they think that if it's on TV, then it must be okay, so they go out and do the same thing, and the results can be tragic to the people and the animals. Even if the public doesn't exactly imitate the activities they've seen on TV and in books, they tend to become overconfident when approaching bears and other wild animals."

CHUCK BARTLEBAUGH

One wildlife celebrity who caught Chuck's eye was a young man named Timothy Treadwell. Chuck first learned of Timothy while on an Alaska Airlines flight after photographing brown bears in Hyder, Alaska. While idly flipping through an in-house magazine, he found a feature article about how Treadwell could get close to wild grizzly bears in remote parts of Alaska. Bartlebaugh thought, *Just what the bears don't need—an article about how to get close to bears in* Alaska Airlines Magazine *read by thousands of people going to Alaska.*

One of CWI's programs is to monitor TV nature programs for inappropriate actions around wildlife. When they began monitoring Treadwell's media appearances, they were shocked at what they found, specifically Timothy Treadwell approaching, touching, and following bears into dense brush.

In 1997 Bartlebaugh tuned in to the *Tom Snyder Show* and groaned when he saw a blond-haired man named Timothy Treadwell purposely moving within a few feet of large grizzly bears in Alaska's Katmai National Park, all the while crooning, "I love you. I love you." Treadwell had recently written the book *Among Grizzlies,* which promoted his disturbing theory that grizzly bears were not as dangerous as people were led to believe, and that with trust and love the great bears would eventually accept a human's close presence (despite the fact that this theory was universally condemned by bear experts and state and federal wildlife management agencies).

Bartlebaugh immediately got on the phone and complained to the producers of the *Tom Snyder Show.* Then he phoned Timothy Treadwell and informed him that he was giving an inappropriate message to the public. "Tim was defensive and testy at first when I confronted him," Bartlebaugh recalled, "but then he backed off and became apologetic, saying that he didn't mean to misinform people, that he just wanted to show that bears weren't dangerous."

Bartlebaugh's phone call to Timothy opened a line of communication between the two men that appeared to bear fruit. Bartlebaugh succeeded in getting Treadwell to stop airing some of his most up-close footage. "I had to fight tooth and nail to stop the NBC *Dateline* program from rerunning the Treadwell segment," Bartlebaugh said, "but they finally agreed to cancel it after I vigorously insisted that they contact the superintendent of Katmai National Park before airing it."

Over the next two years, Timothy Treadwell's behavior became so outrageous in public and on television nature programs—touching and even kissing a bear—that Deb Liggett, superintendent of Katmai National Park, asked if Bartlebaugh would assist Treadwell in developing a responsible wildlife safety message for his school programs.

In March 2000 Chuck Bartlebaugh answered the phone in his office and was surprised to hear Timothy Treadwell's voice. "Tim was real subdued," Bartlebaugh stated. "Katmai National Park officials were threatening to kick him out of the park." Bartlebaugh met Treadwell in Colorado and hammered out a program.

In turn Treadwell promised Bartlebaugh that he would no longer send mixed messages to the public about safety around bears. Bartlebaugh waited and waited for the photos. Finally, he phoned Treadwell, who now wanted to delay the program another year. "I did all that work for nothing," Bartlebaugh said with rising ire. "We were so close to bringing legitimacy to Timothy Treadwell, but he got his head turned by Hollywood film producers who promised him stardom."

Sadly, Timothy Treadwell's rising star was extinguished on the rain-swept afternoon of October 5, 2003, when one or more grizzly bears killed and ate him, along with his girlfriend, Amie Huguenard. Investigating rangers killed two aggressive bears they found feeding on the remains.

Through the years, the Center for Wildlife Information has provided high-quality educational resources and training workshops. Teaching units, videos, CD-ROMs, and slide programs offer a clear visual message to the public on appropriate safety techniques. In addition CWI has also distributed hundreds of thousands of color brochures to further educate the public, with topics that range from telling the difference between black and grizzly bears to safe camping practices in bear country.

And in response to an alarming increase in injuries and loss of human and animal life caused by the actions of misinformed visitors to local and national forests, parks, and wildlife refuges, CWI created the successful Be Bear Aware and Wildlife Stewardship Campaign.

The campaign furnishes the highest quality visual and print media to the public, to youth group leaders for organizations such as the Girl Scouts and Boy Scouts, and to schools so that young people can learn the latest safety techniques for avoiding encounters with bears, mountain lions, and other wild animals and so they can in turn share what they've learned with others. By mustering the support and cooperation of a plethora of agencies—the National Park Service, the U.S. Forest Service, the U.S. Fish & Wildlife Service, the Wildlife Society, and other state and federal wildlife land management agencies—CWI has made a huge impact on the conservation of bears, especially the grizzly.

As a result of such exemplary accomplishments, the CWI has received a host of illustrious awards, including recognition and acknowledgment from the Interagency Grizzly Bear Committee, the Yellowstone Ecosystem Subcommittee, Congressional awards, plus a letter of appreciation from President George H.W. Bush in 1992.

For almost three decades Chuck Bartlebaugh and the Center for Wildlife Information have steadfastly fulfilled its mission of developing educational material for the general public and for instructors about the impact humans have on wild animals and their environment. CWI's mission is critical if the grizzly is to remain a part of our western wilderness. Even though the great bear's survival at times appears to be a very complex issue, a CWI bumper sticker reminds us that the answer remains simple: WILDLIFE + DISTANCE = SAFETY.

CHAPTER 10

·+··━┽━· ·+··+· ━┽━· ·+··+· ━┽━· ·+·

DOUG PEACOCK

SEARCHING FOR SANITY AND
UNDERSTANDING AMONG GRIZZLIES

A lot of people believed that Doug Peacock, emotionally ravaged by his tenure in Vietnam as a Special Forces medic, was hell-bent on destruction during the 1980s when he roamed the backcountry of Glacier National Park, searching for sanity and understanding among grizzlies. But in retrospect I was the one who seemed hell-bent on destruction as I hiked briskly up the 5-mile-long trail in the dark toward the Huckleberry Mountain lookout tower in September 1984.

I was a budding wildlife photographer without the necessary tools to safely create the close-up color images of grizzly bears that magazine editors desired. Carrying a woefully inadequate 200-millimeter telephoto lens attached to a Minolta camera, my plan was to arrive at the huckleberry patches below the lookout tower at first light, a place I'd been told grizzlies, congregated. My goal was to get full body photos of grizzlies and hopefully even some frontal head shots. That I would have to get within 20 yards of a grizzly to accomplish this feat was lost on me, including the fact that I was tripping over huge piles of bear scat along the trail. As I look back on that insane hike through dense forest in the lower reaches of the trail, I believe the only thing that saved my life was the fact that most of bears had migrated to berry patches higher up the mountain.

I broke out of the timber and strode through the first alpine meadow at dawn. Despite my having hiked at breakneck speed up the

169

5-mile trail that rose 3,000 feet in elevation, only a sheen of perspiration clung to my brow. I may have been young and dumb, but at least I was in good shape.

The first rays of sunlight burst over Watchtower Mountain to the east and illuminated the glass window panes of the lookout tower, perched on a rocky bench a quarter-mile away. At this point in my reckless journey I actually began to proceed with caution. I'd been warned the night before at the Belton Bar by a gaunt, sallow-faced stranger clad in grungy military camouflage fatigues. After I'd bought the guy a drink (which, in his condition, he didn't need) and asked where it was that a young man hell-bent on destruction might find the mighty grizzly bear, the guy told me about the huckleberry fields below the lookout tower. His words of caution were not directed toward the grizzlies, but the "crazy son-of-a-bitch" who manned the lookout.

A short, bewhiskered man with a full head of shaggy brown hair was loading his arms with firewood at the base of the lookout tower. "Whoa!" he called after casting a brief glance in my direction. "What the f___k are you doing up here so early?"

I'd barely begun my prideful explanation about hiking through the dark, when this man, who'd introduced himself as Doug Peacock, cut me off with the words, "Run into any griz on your way up?" Before I could reply, he chuckled and added the cryptic remark, "Of course you didn't. Otherwise you wouldn't be here."

Peacock invited me into the lookout tower and began pointing out grizzlies feeding on berry patches along the steep north-facing slopes high above Camas Road. At times six different bears were visible. Peacock pointed to a bear 150 yards below, chomping on huckleberry bushes beside a small meadow and said, "That's a young sow with cubs. She runs from everything." Then, as if realizing that a little knowledge in the hands of a man hell-bent on destruction could be dangerous, he added, "Stay the f___k away from the sows. No telling what state they're in. The boars are always after the cubs. That's why the sows are half nuts all the time."

Peacock then turned his attention to a huge, dark-colored grizzly amiably stripping berry bushes 200 yards away at the head of a narrow side draw. "Man, what a bear that one is!" Peacock exclaimed. "He's a big old boar. He figures the whole mountain is his. Yesterday a big bull moose came over the ridge, and that old bear chased the damn moose almost all the way down to the Camas Road. You walk into that bear, you're in trouble." The phone rang, and Peacock busied himself with technical fire talk, so I excused myself and hurried down the steps.

I eased down through dense brush off to the west side of the rocky ledge, anxious to snap some photos. I'd gone only 40 yards when a tremendous bawl ripped through the crisp morning air, followed by threatening huffs and breaking brush. In a panic I sought safety, but the tallest tree was a stunted hemlock 5 feet tall. I was contemplating wedging myself under a tiny bedrock ledge when a sow grizzly and two cubs burst into the open on a grassy knoll 40 yards away. The bear stopped and whirled, searching for the intruder while her cubs stood on their hind legs, staring at their mother in confusion. The look on the sow's face was a mix of terror and hysterical anger that raised the hair on the back of my neck. Of course, that did not stop me from snapping several photos. Fortunately, the sow did not see me, and a few seconds later she dove into the brush with her cubs scampering close behind.

I spent the rest of the day trying to become a statistic, with only a few distant, blurry images of grizzlies to show for my foolish efforts. As the sun dipped low on the horizon, I stopped by the lookout tower to say goodbye. Doug was on the phone, so I just waved farewell before hurrying down the trail to my pickup.

In time the shaggy-haired man I had met at the lookout tower on Huckleberry Mountain would become famous, his name synonymous with militant grizzly-bear activism. But even back in those early years, Doug Peacock had earned a reputation around Glacier as a grizzly-bear activist on the lunatic fringe. There was the time he noticed a newcomer sitting alone at the Belton Bar, where Peacock and several other militant grizzly bear activists hung out. Peacock walked up to the man and growled, "Who the f___k are you?"

"I'm with the Border Grizzly Project," the man proudly explained. "We're studying . . . "

DOUG PEACOCK

"Just leave the f____g grizzlies alone." Doug punctuated his epithet with a warning jab of his finger.

Before he arrived in Glacier country, Doug Peacock had spent a few years roaming the Yellowstone backcountry communing with griz and, apparently, harassing park rangers. He criticized their disgraceful policy of feeding bears at garbage dumps, and lax enforcement of hunting outfitters south of the park, men who still treated grizzlies as vermin and shot them. The spring after I'd met Peacock at the Huckleberry lookout, I was roaming the open ridges below Dunraven Pass in Yellowstone when a lady ranger strode up and inspected my backpack for elk antlers, which people were in the habit of snitching and selling, against park rules.

The ranger asked if I'd seen any grizzlies. I told her I hadn't, then mentioned the remarkable visit I'd had with a park employee manning a lookout tower in Glacier named Doug Peacock.

The ranger sniffed and commented, "Oh yeah, we know all about Doug Peacock. He's got the right name—Peacock. He thinks he knows everything about grizzly bears, but he doesn't know enough to keep from getting himself killed. He'll probably be the next bear lover who gets mauled. We ran him out of this country, and I for one say good riddance. Glacier can have him."

I have no idea what precipitated her tirade against Peacock, though it may have been one of his patented offhand comments like, "leave the f____g grizzlies alone."

Peacock's remarkable association with the grizzly began on a most desperate note in March 1968. Forty-eight hours after dodging bullets and patching body parts as a Green Beret medic in Vietnam, a bewildered, frustrated, angry, and dangerous Doug Peacock was deposited in his small hometown in Michigan. Like so many other Vietnam vets, Peacock may have been out of the war, but the war wasn't out of him.

With images of sticky hot blood and the screams and moans of dying men flitting through his mind, Peacock loaded his old pickup with camping gear and a wrinkled old map and headed West to fulfill

Doug Peacock holding his cat, Elk

his destiny. For it had been that map, of Wyoming and Montana, that had kept him somewhat sane during the madness of Vietnam. Every night he would spread the map out and study it, with the hope that if he somehow survived the nightmare of the war, he would seek out the solitude of those wild places his grimy finger traced on the map.

Peacock kept to himself as he wandered aimlessly through the West, occasionally visiting civilization to buy food or demolish a pay phone booth with a .357 magnum pistol for the offense of requesting payment, as mentioned in his book *Grizzly Years*. The wandering provided diversion but did little to ease his pain. Every conscious thought was of Vietnam, and even drinking himself into oblivion at night couldn't keep the nightmares at bay.

Eventually Peacock migrated to Yellowstone and sought out the isolated areas he had been daydreaming about. One afternoon he spotted a sow grizzly with cubs just 150 yards away. The animals were coming toward him, and Peacock, gripped by a surge of fear, scrambled up a tree, for he'd heard that grizzlies attacked every human they encountered but couldn't climb. To his amazement, the bears passed 40 feet from the tree and ignored him.

After the bears had gone, Peacock climbed down the tree, and when his feet struck the ground, a searing pain shot up both legs. Remarkably, the fear and the pain in his body caused a quickening in his spirit—a powerful reminder that he was truly alive and that maybe there was some reason to go on living. As he sat huddled near a campfire that night, for the first time since he'd come home from the war, his thoughts were not on blood squirting in his face from a ruptured aorta or the bloated bodies of children floating in rice paddies. Like a healing salve to his mind and soul, his reflections instead were on the big female grizzly and her two cubs—something out there in the night to fear and respect that was not an enemy.

The next day Peacock spotted a large boar grizzly and two lesser bears, one of which was a sow with two tiny cubs. He followed them at a distance, noting what they fed on, where they traveled, where they bedded. That night he dreamed of bears and sunlight and fresh air and wildflowers.

Peacock eventually migrated north to Glacier, and there discovered a place made just for him. It's called the Trapline, a lonely stretch of highway just west of Glacier National Park dotted with seedy bars that beckoned a menagerie of lowlifes and people who didn't want to be found. It's an easy place to get into trouble if a person isn't careful. Peacock fit right in with the Trapline crowd, many of whom were Vietnam vets attracted by the area's remoteness and its reputation as a place where the law was mostly absent and people could do whatever they damn well pleased.

But Glacier's habitat was far different from Yellowstone's gently rolling sage-covered hills where a hiker can see a bear a mile away. Glacier country was ruggedly steep and choked with brush, with giant snow-capped peaks rising to the sky like giant, brooding sentinels. However the grizzlies remained the same—amiable and contented when left alone, unpredictable and fearsome when encountered at close range.

Peacock's considerable experience with bears at close range in Yellowstone, and later in Glacier, began to pay dividends as he slowly began to understand the great bear's behavior. He became convinced that travel in grizzly country could be relatively safe if a hiker took precautions to avoid surprising a grizzly at close range, the leading cause of bear attacks. But after several charging bears veered off when Peacock stood his ground, he became convinced that an advancing grizzly was still in the process of deciding if it wanted to break off the charge or pummel the source of its ire, and a person's actions while the bear charged were oftentimes the deciding factor between a near mauling and a real mauling. Peacock came to believe a person had to show that his or her intentions were nonthreatening without showing weakness. He became adamantly opposed to running for a tree and trying to climb it, something few people are adept at. Such an action, Peacock claims, is sure to trigger a predatory response in a bear that might otherwise have broken off its charge.

A good illustration of Peacock's technique occurred while he was hiking down through a steep, narrow lake outlet when he spotted a medium-sized grizzly feeding on a terrace about 50 yards below. Peacock called to the bear, but the roar of the cascading waterfall drowned out his voice. So he kicked a rock loose, at the same time waving his arms. The bear looked up, spotted Peacock and ran a short distance away, but skidded to a halt before turning back and rearing up.

For several seconds man and bear stared at each other. Peacock was just beginning to breathe easy when the bear dropped to all fours, and with his head lowered, charged. Startled but determined to show no sign of weakness, he waved his arms again and spoke even louder. The bear came to an abrupt halt by aggressively slamming his front paws on the ground. Peacock called out to the bear, and the animal responded with another short charge. Though the bear was getting uncomfortably close, Peacock stood his ground and continued talking in a low voice while averting his eyes. The grizzly made another short hopping charge but stopped. After a few seconds, the bear broke eye contact by looking off to the side, then spun around and galloped out of sight down the steep gully.

In times of frustration with what he perceived as inadequate federal bear management, Peacock has claimed to be an anarchist. But then he got an offer he couldn't refuse and actually joined the establishment, taking a job with the National Park Service as a seasonal fire lookout atop Huckleberry Mountain, located along the western edge of the park just 3 miles from the town of West Glacier. Peacock soon learned that Huckleberry Mountain was aptly named, with the subalpine side hills below the lookout tower covered with berry bushes.

That first August in the park, with the berries turning ripe, Doug looked out one morning and was excited to see a grizzly 80 yards below the tower stripping berries, leaves, and stems. Another grizzly arrived the next day, then another, and by the first week in September he could often see a dozen grizzlies feeding. There were little bears, big bears, sows with cubs, teenage bears. And a few dominant males, one of which was the surly black grizzly. If there was a heaven on earth, Peacock had found it. He called his little piece of paradise the Grizzly Hilton and joked that the government was actually paying him to live among the great bears.

He was in his fifth year as a fire lookout when I met him. Two years later, he felt he needed a change. He gave up his job on Huckleberry Mountain and began writing about his life and the bears he knew. From his labors grew the book *Grizzly Years,* which chronicled his evolution from a rage-filled Vietnam vet to a man at peace in the wilderness with the great bear. The book struck a cord with a vast army of people who were themselves aimlessly wandering through life.

The book catapulted Peacock into the limelight as an eco-warrior and one of the most knowledgeable authorities on grizzly bears. Fame had never been one of Peacock's goals in life, nor did he accept it when offers for speaking engagements began pouring in, preferring instead the solitude of the Yellowstone backcountry. However, Peacock eventually recognized the opportunity to deliver to the public his message of appreciation and conservation of the grizzly. One speaking engagement led to another and another, until Peacock today has grown somewhat accepting of his place among the elite conservationists in the bear world.

That doesn't mean Peacock lost his edge as a warrior for the grizzly's cause. In the early 1990s he led two expeditions into Colorado's South San Juan Mountains in search of evidence of grizzly bears. As mentioned in chapter 1, the San Juans were rumored to harbor a few grizzlies. State wildlife officials steadfastly denied the grizzly's existence, but they'd already been proven wrong once, when hunting guide Ed Wiseman was mauled by a twenty-two-year-old sow grizzly before he killed the bear. The female had borne cubs, and had been mated by at least one boar. Where were they?

Peacock's expedition produced several huge piles of bear scat that were too big to have come from a black bear, along with a few grizzly-like hairs, and photographic evidence of recent digs (places where grizzlies dig up ground squirrels and marmots). However, state officials rejected this evidence because it had not been furnished by a recognized wildlife biologist. (Hence, Peacock's occasional tirade about being an anarchist.)

The enormity of Doug Peacock's appeal to the ecology-minded is best illustrated by a 2003 writer's conference I was invited to participate in at the Montana Festival of the Book, which brings in accomplished fiction and nonfiction writers to share insights on their craft. I sat on a panel titled "Writing About Grizzly Bears," which consisted of noted bear writer Roland Cheek, *Outside* magazine contributor David Quaman, Doug Peacock, and myself.

The audience packed the room and sat patiently while Cheek, Quaman, and I took turns sharing our thoughts on the ethics and responsibility of writing about a potentially dangerous animal like the grizzly. When Peacock took the podium, the audience rose to its feet and cheered. He did not disappoint the faithful, for he spoke with a subtle passion and eloquence of his hopes and fears concerning the plight of the grizzly, and ended his talk by urging the audience to do its part in protecting the grizzly remnant from the ravages of narrow-minded men. Not surprisingly, most of the questions from the audience were directed at Doug.

One man stood at the back of the room and asked, "Hey Doug, where's the Grizzly Hilton located that you wrote about in your book?"

Peacock shook his head and replied, "Can't tell you. Wouldn't matter if I did anyway. It's gone forever."

Later, as Peacock and I chatted about our meeting almost twenty years earlier (he swore he remembered me), I asked what he meant by his remark about the Grizzly Hilton being gone. He fumed.

> Hell, they burned it up back in 2000. They torched Huckleberry Mountain as a backfire, supposedly to save the town of West Glacier. Hell, the town wasn't in danger of burning up. It was all some crazy bureaucrat's wild idea. They burned up the whole damn mountain. I hiked up there this summer, and all those huckleberry patches below the lookout tower are gone. The place is just a charred heap of rock. They oughta change its name to Burnt Peak. There won't be any huckleberries up there for twenty years. I don't know what the grizzlies are gonna do for berries.

One of Doug Peacock's greatest contributions to the grizzly's cause has been his emphasis on the role of everyday people in grizzly bear conservation. Following Peacock's example, many thousands of bear lovers have become vocal proponents of the grizzly and its habitat. And Peacock's not done making waves, either. He has laid his cameras aside, claiming that he is through stressing bears by moving in on them and that from now on he intends to sit and watch them at a distance that's safe for both man and bear. If that's the work of an anarchist, we could all use a little more of such anarchy.

CONCLUSION

JUST LEAVE THE @#%$& GRIZZLIES ALONE!

Can you imagine the wake-up call the bear researcher at the Belton Bar got the evening Doug Peacock walked up to him and spouted his classic epithet: "Just leave the @#%$& grizzlies alone." That researcher may not have realized it, but he received in a single expletive-laced outburst the accumulated wisdom of all those who came before and after him.

There is very little chance that most of us will ever take part in a scientific endeavor concerning the grizzly, but we can, like Doug Peacock, become part of the new nonexclusive army of conservationists who preach that very simple yet foolproof doctrine: Leave the grizzly alone.

There are several ways to accomplish this goal. The most obvious is to stay away from any grizzly in the wild. Bears don't like surprises, and they don't like to be pressured. It scares them. They have no way of understanding that many people view them with love and appreciation; they believe instead that all two-legged intruders have the potential to be dangerous, so they attack before they're attacked.

Bear experts have learned that when a human moves within 60 yards of a grizzly, he or she penetrates the bear's comfort zone, which may prompt an aggressive reaction. I've been there. It's no fun. But guess what? Standing back 200 yards from every grizzly virtually eliminates the danger. Personally, I like to stay back about 400 yards, or a quarter mile. That way, if a bear begins moving in my direction, I can slip away without it ever knowing I was there.

At seminars whenever I preach the doctrine: BEARS + DISTANCE = SAFETY, someone always jumps up and counters, "But what if you stumble into a grizzly on a trail?"

Yeah, it's happened to me. Through no fault of mine or the grizzly's, man and bear do occasionally meet at an uncomfortably close range. Climbing a tree is no option. Studies show the average time span before a surprised bear attacks an intruder is 2.9 seconds. That's not enough time to climb a tree, and it's barely enough time to curl up into the fetal position and hope the bear merely delivers a few cuffs before retreating. Even then, a few swats from a grizzly are usually enough to scar a person for life.

A few years ago a man and woman were hiking in Glacier National Park when they encountered a grizzly at close range. They dropped onto their bellies and laid with their hands clasped over the backs of their necks, a position that would protect their vital organs. The grizzly sniffed the man and then the woman. Almost as an afterthought the bear bit the woman on the right buttock, removing a five-pound chunk of muscle.

There's no reason for a person to be subjected to such terror and torment. It doesn't have to happen this way. If that man and woman had carried bear spray, a short burst of airborne red pepper would most likely have sent that charging bear in hasty retreat. Despite the proven success rate (90 percent against attacking bears) of bear spray, I am dumbfounded by the number of hikers I encounter in Glacier and Yellowstone blissfully striding along trails in grizzly country without it. My own survey shows only one in ten hikers carries the stuff. This is not only dangerous, it's irresponsible. It is a sad fact that when a bear attacks a human, it is often hunted down later and killed by authorities. I carry my can of bear spray everywhere I go in bear and mountain-lion country. The stuff is lightweight, easy to use, and costs less than a tank of gas.

One more way we can preach the doctrine of bear safety is to share what we know. My friend Roland Dixon was in a sporting goods store when he heard a man ask the salesman about the best pistol to purchase for protection against bears. Roland explained the value of using bear spray instead of deadly force, and he won the guy over.

Another good idea is to get behind the Center for Wildlife Information's Be Bear Aware Campaign. Most bear problems are caused by ignorance and fear, and CWI's pamphlets, brochures, quick-reference cards, and bumper stickers are excellent educational tools for schoolchildren, hikers, and recreationists living in bear country.

The greatest danger to the grizzly today, in my opinion, is the current trend on television nature programs to reinvent the grizzly as a kinder, gentler animal. Several recent nature programs have shown humans approaching and even touching grizzlies. Timothy Treadwell, who was often shown moving to within mere feet of grizzlies, sometimes even touching them, while crooning, "I love you. I love you." Treadwell believed the grizzly was misunderstood and that man and beast could eventually form a bond of trust. If the proof is in the pudding, Treadwell was wrong. He and Amie were killed and eaten by one or more brown grizzly bears in 2003.

As enlightened advocates for the grizzly, we must respond in loud and militant fashion, like Doug Peacock, protesting to TV networks that showing people acting improperly around grizzlies is wrong. We need to scream that when people move in close to a grizzly, it habituates the bear to humans, which is usually a precursor to the bear's death. We must remind the TV execs that the two bears found feeding on Treadwell's remains were shot and killed by authorities.

The grizzly bear has been studied to death. We know what it eats, where it sleeps, what makes it burp, etc. These studies were necessary and useful in understanding grizzly physiology and formulating management plans for the great bear. But it hasn't stopped the killing. People are still doing dumb things in bear country that get themselves and the bears injured or killed.

It's up to us to educate people about carrying bear spray and maintaining a safe distance. What an extraordinary privilege it is to carry the message of respect and temperance passed on by grizzled old men like Bud Cheff and Howard Copenhaver, Bud Moore, John and

CONCLUSION

Frank Craighead, and Chuck Jonkel. Nor can we overlook the great sacrifices of Carrie Hunt, Chuck Bartlebaugh, and Doug Peacock.

Of course, every army needs a slogan. How about: Just leave the grizzlies alone!

Bear safety is not rocket science. There are two basic rules of proper behavior in bear country that are simple yet foolproof: Leave the bears alone, and carry bear spray. One precludes an encounter, the other precludes an incident.

With startling efficiency civilized man has conquered one "last frontier" after another. Outer space, that endless string of galaxies stretching into infinity, was once thought to be the last frontier. We did more than conquer it; we traveled through it, invaded its planets, and proved that no matter how far outer space extended, it was really just a bunch of frozen rocks devoid of life. So why bother?

Then came the Internet, reducing 10,000 miles to a nanosecond and furnishing the human race with dominion over time and distance, providing the world with an instant form of communication. And with the help of DNA, we can literally recreate ourselves in our own image. Truly, we've become our own gods.

And yet, there remains a niggling problem with our ascendancy to godliness: We have not yet managed to subdue the savage beast. Oh, we've done all right in that area through the ages, what with domesticating some wild animals and eliminating those that bared their fangs. But we really haven't tamed the savage beast, especially the big predators. We've trapped them, shot them, exterminated them, but we really haven't conquered their wildness. The tiger may be caged, but God help the human who enters its cage demanding submission.

In America the grizzly has remained that sort of conundrum since Lewis and Clark first encountered its adverse reaction to their musket balls along the banks of the Missouri River. The grizzly simply refuses to lose its wildness. It maintains its indifference to our best of intentions to reinvent it as a kinder, gentler animal and maybe take away some of that primal instinct that scares us.

BIBLIOGRAPHY

BOOKS

Bass, Rick. *The Lost Grizzlies: A Search for Survivors in the Wilderness of Colorado*. New York: Houghton Mifflin, 1995.

Brown, David. *The Grizzly in the Southwest*. Norman, Okla.: University of Oklahoma Press, 1985.

Cheff, Bud. *Indian Trails and Grizzly Tales*. Stevensville, Mont.: Stoneydale Press, 1993.

Copenhaver, Howard. *They Left Their Tracks*. Stevensville, Mont.: Stoneydale Press, 1990.

Fritz, Jean. *Bully for You, Teddy Roosevelt!* New York: Putnam, 1991.

Leopold, Aldo. *A Sand County Almanac*. New York: Random House, 1996.

Moore, Bud. *The Lochsa Story*. Missoula, Mont.: Mountain Press, 1995.

Morris, Edmund. *Theodore Rex*. New York: Random House, 2001.

Peacock, Doug. *Grizzly Years*. New York: Henry Holt, 1990.

Petersen, David. *Ghost Grizzlies: Does the Great Bear Still Haunt Colorado?* New York: Henry Holt & Company, 1995.

Roosevelt, Teddy. *Hunting the Grizzly and Other Sketches.* New York: Barnes & Noble Books, 2003.

Russell, Andy. *Grizzly Country.* New York: Lyons Press, 1967.

Schneider, Bill. *Where the Grizzly Walks.* Helena, Mont.: The Globe Pequot Press, 2004.

Schullery, Paul. *American Bears.* New York: Roberts Rinehart Publishing, 1997.

———. *The Bears of Yellowstone.* New York: Roberts Rinehart Publishing, 1986.

———. *Lewis & Clark among the Grizzlies.* Helena, Mont.: The Globe Pequot Press, 2002.

Storer, Tracey and Lloyd Tevis Jr. *The California Grizzly.* Berkeley: University of California Press, 1955.

Wright, William. *The Grizzly Bear.* New York: Scribner, 1909.

PUBLISHED RESEARCH PAPERS

Craighead, Frank and John. "A Population Analysis of the Yellowstone Grizzly Bears." Published research paper by the Montana Cooperative Wildlife Research Unit, University of Montana, 1974.

———. "An Ecological Study of the Grizzly Bear." Published research paper by the Montana Cooperative Wildlife Research Unit, University of Montana, 1963.

———. "Management of Bears in Yellowstone National Park." Published research paper by the Montana Cooperative Wildlife Research Unit, University of Montana, 1967.

BIBLIOGRAPHY

———. "Radio Tracking Grizzly Bears." Published research paper by the Montana Cooperative Wildlife Research Unit, University of Montana, 1963.

Craighead, John. "A Delineation of Critical Grizzly Bear Habitat in the Yellowstone Region." Published research paper by the Montana Cooperative Wildlife Research Unit, University of Montana, 1977.

Hunt, Carrie. "Bear Deterrent Tests." Published research paper by Northern Border Grizzly Research Study, 1982.

Hunt, Hammond, Peterson, Carriles. "Aversive Conditioning Study." Published research paper by the Wyoming Game and Fish Department, 1988.

Hunt and Smith. "Repellents and Deterrents for Black and Grizzly Bears." Published research paper by the Northern Border Grizzly Research Study, 1983.

Jonkel, Charles. "A Delineation of Grizzly Bear Habitat in the Border Grizzly Area." Published research paper by the Northern Border Grizzly Research Study, 1976.

———. "Border Grizzly Project Annual Report Number One." Published research paper by the Northern Border Grizzly Research Study, 1976.

———. "Border Grizzly Project Annual report Number Two." Published research paper by the Northern Border Grizzly Research Study, 1977.

———. "Border Grizzly Project Annual Report Number Three." Published research paper by the Northern Border Grizzly Research Study, 1978.

———. "Border Grizzly Project Annual Report Number Four." Published research paper by the Northern Border Grizzly Research Study, 1979.

BIBLIOGRAPHY

————. "Border Grizzly Project Five Year Summary Report." Published research paper by the Northern Border Grizzly Reseach Study, 1982.

————. "Mexican Grizzly Studies." Published research paper by the Northern Border Grizzly Research Study, 1978.

ARTICLES

Associated Press. "Mountain Lions Poisoned." *The Arizona Republic.* February 6, 2005.

Dawson, Donald. "Bear Dogs on Patrol for Problem Grizzlies." www.nationalgeographic.com. July 18, 2002.

Hunt, Carrie. "Bear Shepherding Guidelines for Safe and Effective Treatment of Human-Bear Conflicts." www.beardogs.org.

————. "Partners-in-Life" Program. Wind River Bear Institute. www.bear dogs.org.

Jamison, Michael. "A Grizzly Proposition." *Wildlife Journal.* Spring 2001.

Pole, Joyce and Peter Tyack. "Elephants Learn by Sounds Mimicry." BBCNEWS.COM. March 24, 2005.

ABOUT THE AUTHOR

Mike Lapinski is the award-winning author of twelve outdoor and nature books and hundreds of magazine articles. His wildlife photos have appeared as inside and cover art in a variety of magazines and books. Mike is also the host of numerous outdoor and nature video programs.

Mike is considered an expert on the use of bear pepper spray. He often speaks on this subject and on bears and self-defense for nature lovers. Mike lives with his wife, Aggie, in the heart of the Rockies in Superior, Montana.